LABOUR SAVING GARDENING

LABOUR SAVING GARDENING

Oliver Dawson

Galley Press

Contents

First published in Great Britain in 1980 by
Octopus Books Limited

This edition published in 1988 by
Galley Press
in association with
Octopus Books
Michelin House, 81 Fulham Road
London SW3 6RB

ISBN 0 86136 062 1

Printed by Mandarin Offset in Hong Kong

Introduction

This book will show you how to cut down on the time and labour spent on making and caring for your garden, without sacrificing interest and beauty. In fact, many of the short cuts described here will result in a marked improvement in its appearance.

No garden worthy of the name, however, has been made or maintained without a certain amount of hard work, and it would be foolish, and indeed dishonest, to claim otherwise. As Rudyard Kipling wrote: 'Gardens are not made by singing "Oh! How beautiful!" and sitting in the shade.' Everyone who wants an attractive garden should realize that there are certain basic routine jobs that cannot be avoided. I have tried to show you how to carry out these tasks with minimum effort and maximum efficiency.

For this purpose, a new approach to gardening is needed, ranging right through from the initial planning to planting and maintenance. We must avoid tackling garden chores in a certain way because 'that's the way they have always been done'. Careful planning is of particular importance, and some time spent on this will save many hours work later, as it is far easier to introduce new features to a garden than to get rid of established ones.

Even in the smallest of gardens, the work load can be greatly lightened by taking advantage of the many labour-saving mechanized gardening tools now available. Power-driven mowers, hedge trimmers, cultivators and various other tools have all made a great contribution in this connection. It pays to buy the best quality tools you can afford, as these should not only last longer, but also be easier to use and require less maintenance.

Garden centres, with their takeaway container-grown material, have helped gardeners to appreciate the value of a whole new range of plants. Shrubs, in particular, are great labour-savers. They are long term, trouble-free garden investments that declare annual dividends in the shape of beautiful flowers, fruit and foliage. Perennials, chosen for their labour-saving qualities, provide colour throughout the seasons. Ground-cover plants will smother weeds while making their contribution to the overall beauty of the garden; like the perennials, they require little attention once established.

You can cut down on work in the kitchen garden by a suitable choice of crops. The section on vegetable growing lays special emphasis on vegetables that are relatively trouble-free, as well as those that provide supplies for the table over a long period without extra work being involved.

So, whether your spare time is restricted, or whether you are elderly, infirm or just plain lazy, there is no reason why you shouldn't have a garden of which you can be proud without spending more time and effort on its construction and upkeep than you want to.

The labour-intensive garden

- Narrow path between house and garden means that the edges of the lawn will become badly worn, particularly in bad weather, and mud and dirt will be tramped into the house.
- Not enough space to sit out on paved area when the grass is wet or to display plants in tubs attractively.
- Too many annuals and bedding plants which need constant attention.
- Too many small beds in the lawn make mowing difficult.
- Lawn edges need regular trimming.
- Grass round base of tree trunks will need hand clipping.
- Border plants overhanging the lawn make mowing difficult.
- Dead leaves, grass, weeds and debris will collect in space between path and lawn.
- Beech tree will grow much too large for this type of garden and the roots will take too many nutrients out of the soil. The overhanging branches will cast too much shade.
- Apple tree is too crowded in by other plants which will affect size of crop and increase risk of pests and diseases.
- Privet hedge will need regular trimming.
- Border plants grown so close to the wall will need extra watering, particularly in dry hot weather.
- Gaps between plants encourage weeds.
- Bare, exposed soil quickly dries out in hot or windy weather.
- Grass path creates unnecessary work and provides insufficient access to crops; it also becomes worn and muddy in wet weather.
- No proper provision for crop rotation. Poor planning results in wasted effort and poor returns, as well as encouraging a build-up of pests and diseases.
- Fruit trees are poorly sited and take up valuable space; overhanging branches cast shade.
- Soft fruit bushes have no protection from birds.
- No compost heap.
- Nowhere to store garden tools.

8

The labour-saving garden

- Patio provides valuable and attractive recreation area (for greater detail see page 23).
- Annuals and bedding plants have been replaced by easy-care perennials and shrubs.
- The small beds in the lawn have been removed making mowing both quicker and easier.
- Paving slabs between border and lawn prevent plants damaging the grass and encouraging weeds and moss. It also prevents plants from being caught in the mower and eliminates edge cutting by hand.
- Gentle curves to lawn edges make mowing easier.
- Long hedge has been replaced by low maintenance fencing which also provides support for climbing shrubs.
- Ground cover plants suppress weeds and when established will eliminate this time-consuming chore.
- Thick mulch conserves moisture and suppresses weeds.
- Self-clinging climbers and wall shrubs require little attention and brighten up the long expanse of wall and fence.
- Beech tree is replaced by birch, which is more suited to a small garden.

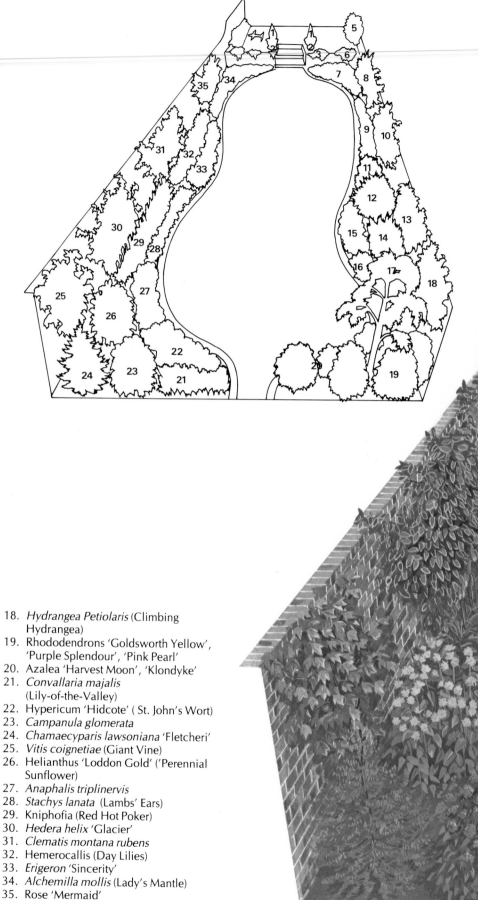

Key:
1. *Chamaecyparis lawsoniana* 'Nana' (Dwarf Cypress)
2. Lobelia
3. *Oxalis inops* (Wood Sorrel)
4. *Juniperus x media*
5. *Chaenomeles speciosa*
6. *Hedera colchica dentata* 'Variegata' (Giant Ivy)
7. *Monarda* 'Croftway Pink' (Bergamot)
8. *Clematis* 'Nelly Moser'
9. *Geum* 'Mrs Bradshaw'
10. *Lonicera periclymenum* (Honeysuckle)
11. *Eryngium* (Sea Holly)
12. *Robinia hispida* 'Silver Queen'
13. *Euonymus fortunei radicans* 'Silver Queen'
14. Solidago 'Goldenmosa' (Golden Rod)
15. Sedum 'Autumn Joy'
16. *Potentilla atrosanguinea* 'Gibson's Scarlet'
17. *Betula Pendula Youngii* (Young's Weeping Birch)
18. *Hydrangea Petiolaris* (Climbing Hydrangea)
19. Rhododendrons 'Goldsworth Yellow', 'Purple Splendour', 'Pink Pearl'
20. Azalea 'Harvest Moon', 'Klondyke'
21. *Convallaria majalis* (Lily-of-the-Valley)
22. Hypericum 'Hidcote' (St. John's Wort)
23. *Campanula glomerata*
24. *Chamaecyparis lawsoniana* 'Fletcheri'
25. *Vitis coignetiae* (Giant Vine)
26. Helianthus 'Loddon Gold' ('Perennial Sunflower)
27. *Anaphalis triplinervis*
28. *Stachys lanata* (Lambs' Ears)
29. Kniphofia (Red Hot Poker)
30. *Hedera helix* 'Glacier'
31. *Clematis montana rubens*
32. Hemerocallis (Day Lilies)
33. *Erigeron* 'Sincerity'
34. *Alchemilla mollis* (Lady's Mantle)
35. Rose 'Mermaid'

1·Basic Techniques

Understanding Your Soil

The type and condition of the soil is one of the most important contributory factors to successful gardening. Soil conditions not only determine the kinds of plants you will be able to grow, but also the amount of time and trouble that you will need to spend in growing them.

It is better to choose plants that suit your soil than to try and change the soil to suit your plants. The latter procedure is seldom worth the considerable effort involved, since there are so many plants worth growing that will flourish in widely differing soil conditions.

Soils range from heavy clays, in which the soil particles are so small that they bind together into a sticky unworkable mass in wet weather, to light sandy soils, whose larger granular structure makes them easy to work under almost any conditions. Chalk soils pose difficult drainage problems and the subsoil, often consisting of solid chalk, will need breaking up to 60 cm (2 ft) or more deep.

With the exception of chalk, which is always alkaline, soils also vary in their degree of acidity or alkalinity. This is measured by what is known as the pH scale. The neutral point on this scale is pH7, which indicates that the soil is neither acid nor alkaline. Readings below pH7 indicate an acid

It is vital to choose plants to suit your soil. The hosta, agapanthus (blue flowers) and Japanese Maple in this attractive labour-saving border will grow in any fertile, well-drained soil, but the rhododendron needs an acid soil.

soil (the lower the pH value, the more acid the soil), while those from pH7 upwards indicate an alkaline one (the higher the pH, the more alkaline the soil). The optimum soil conditions for the majority of garden plants are slightly acid – from pH6 to pH6.5.

Soil-testing kits are obtainable from most garden shops and centres or direct from the manufacturers, who often advertise in gardening magazines. Kits range from simple inexpensive kinds to more elaborate ones which, as well as registering the pH factor, indicate any trace elements and fertilizers that are lacking and specify the amounts needed to make good the deficiency.

Soil-testing kits are a worthwhile investment, because they will save you much frustration and unnecessary work in trying to grow plants that are not suited to your soil conditions. Plants grow much more healthily in the right conditions and this in turn makes them less susceptible to pests and diseases.

Although soils are usually described as belonging to just one of the categories mentioned above (clay, sand, chalk), most garden soils are really a mixture of several types – especially if the plot has been under cultivation for a long time. In larger gardens, too, you will sometimes find different soil types in different parts of the plot. In my own garden, for example, which generally enjoys the benefits of a light acid loam, there is an area of heavy unmanageable clay where the subsoil was excavated for an ornamental pool when the garden was first laid out.

Adding Humus

If you can make the effort and spare the time, you can do much to improve the fertility of your soil by adding materials that are rich in humus; in the long term this will prove to be a labour-saving operation. Humus is a complex organic material in the soil produced by the decay of dead vegetable and animal

Above: Soil-testing kits enable you to identify your soil conditions and help prevent failures. Below: Compost heaps should always be covered to prevent them from becoming wet and soggy.

matter. It has the seemingly paradoxical effect of improving the moisture-holding properties of light soils as well as improving the drainage of heavier soils by coagulating their smaller particles.

The main sources of humus in the garden are animal manures, peat, leaf-mould, compost, bark fibre, spent hops and, for those within easy reach of the seashore, seaweed. Gardeners who live in towns or suburbs may find it difficult to obtain animal manures but garden compost, which can be made easily by any gardener, is an excellent substitute. Recipes for making it are as varied as those of Mrs. Beeton, but they can be reduced to certain basic fundamentals. Almost any material of vegetable origin can be used for composting, including grass clippings, hedge trimmings, dead leaves, annual weeds etc. The house will provide kitchen wastes in the shape of vegetable peelings, tea-leaves, lettuce and cabbage leaves. Even the contents of the vacuum cleaner dust bag and old woollens, cut up into strips, can be used.

Diseased plant material, such as blighted potato leaves, and tough, woody prunings should not be in-

cluded. Together with pernicious perennial weeds such as ground elder, couch grass and bindweed, they should go onto the bonfire. Bonfire ash can be added to the compost heap and is a valuable source of potash (but do not use ash from coal, coke or any other source). The potash content of the ash is quickly washed away by rain, so keep the ash under cover until you put it on the heap.

Smaller quantities of material are best composted in the special plastic or wire containers obtainable for the purpose, or in a home-made bin with slatted wooden sides and a roof to stop rain drenching the heap. Where sufficient space and vegetable waste are available, however, you can build an open heap. You will need about 1 tonne (1 ton) of material and it is best to make the heap in one go. Choose a partly shaded moist site, preferably out of sight of the house windows. If this is impossible, the heap can be camouflaged with a length or two of wattle or interlap fencing. Heaps of this kind should be at least 1.5 m (5 ft) long and of a similar width. An optimum height is 1.2–1.5 m (4–5 ft). The sides of the heap should taper slightly towards the top.

Whether you use a container or

not, the heap should be built directly on the soil – not on a base of stone or concrete. This will allow easy access for earthworms and the various other soil animals and bacteria, which will break down the compost materials, transforming them into sweet-smelling, dark crumbling material, rich in humus. A compost heap should be built up in layers, like a series of sandwiches. The first layer consists of 15–30 cm (6 in–1 ft) of organic wastes, covered by a light layer of soil, followed by a dusting of lime (just enough to whiten the surface). These three layers are repeated until the heap reaches the required height: not more than 1.5 m (5 ft). It is then capped with a 5 cm (2 in) layer of soil to keep the heat in.

The compost will take up to a year to rot down but the process can be speeded up, either by the use of one of the proprietary accelerators or by dressings of sulphate of ammonia at intervals while the heap is under construction. Such additives will also do away with the need for turning the heap and thus cut down on the labour involved.

Stable, farmyard, pigeon or poultry manure also act as accelerators and help to speed up the rotting down process if added to the heap during building. This is a good way of making the best use of organic fertilizers in short supply.

By using compost regularly as a surface dressing or 'mulch', the work of digging and weeding can be reduced. If compost is spread on beds and borders and lightly forked in between plants, there will be no need for deeper or more thorough cultivation. Weeds are suppressed by such a mulch and any that germinate later are easy to pull out, thanks to the light friable texture created.

Digging

Digging can be one of the most back-breaking and time-consuming of garden chores. However, you don't need to go at it like the proverbial bull at a gate, and the deep and thorough digging recommended by many gardening books, although desirable, is not absolutely essential to success. It will usually be sufficient if the topsoil is turned over to a spade's depth when the preliminary preparation of the beds is being carried out. You can use a fork to break up the subsoil beneath as you go.

The choice of suitable tools for the job will help to cut down on the time and effort spent on this task. Buy the best spade and fork you can afford, choosing those that suit your capabilities and that feel 'right' when you handle them. If digging soon tires you, opt for a lady's spade or fork. These days, many gardeners are turning to these lighter and easier models, to the extent that manufacturers are renaming them 'border' spades and forks to save embarrassment to their more chauvinistic male customers. If funds will run to it, always choose tools made of stainless steel, as they are stronger, maintain a sharper edge, and weigh less than other types.

For clay soils, there is a useful type of spade with a curved blade, known as a 'graft'. This makes a sickle-shaped bite into the soil which prevents it sticking to the blade, cutting down on the time spent in scraping off lumps of clay. Grafts are not easy to come by, but for those who garden on heavy clay, tracking down a supplier is well worth the effort.

For the physically handicapped,

Aids to easier digging (left to right): a graft for heavy clay soils; a mechanical spade; and a powered cultivator.

the elderly or infirm or indeed for anyone who wants to take some of the backache out of digging, there are mechanical spades and forks with a kind of lever action which lift and turn the soil in a single operation (see illustration, page 13).

A mechanical cultivator is a worthwhile investment for anyone with a garden of more than 0.2 ha (half an acre) in area. For smaller gardens it is cheaper to hire a machine for the initial preparation of the sites for lawns, beds and borders.

Although these machines save time and labour, bear in mind that they cannot remove the weeds as you do when hand digging; instead, many of the weeds are buried beneath the surface of the soil. Even after a thorough going-over of the plot with the rotavator to chop up the weeds, the more persistent ones will recover and grow again, especially during wet spells. The best time to rotavate, therefore, is in dry weather when there is much less chance of such a re-emergence of weed growth.

In the initial stages of digging, you should incorporate as much organic material as you have available into the top layer of soil. Later, forking in

quantities of compost, peat or other materials rich in humus, supplemented by annual dressings of a general fertilizer, such as 'Growmore', will keep the soil in good condition.

Regular mulching with compost, peat or leafmould will also cut down on the need for digging, since they will help to suppress weeds and need only lightly forking into the topsoil during autumn or winter.

Anything that lightens the soil texture makes cultivation easier, and mulching, which is a sort of composting *in situ*, will improve it to a depth of 30 cm (1 ft) or more as the materials of the mulch are broken down by earthworms and soil bacteria. After a few seasons of regular treatment, even the most difficult plots should end up with a reasonable depth of friable, fertile soil.

No-digging methods

Various garden books nowadays advocate the 'no-digging' system of gardening as a means of saving labour. The initial preparation for a 'no-digging' garden starts, paradoxically, with digging. First, the chosen

plot is dug over to a depth of about 30 cm (1 ft). Annual weeds can be turned in as digging progresses; persistent and deep-rooting weeds such as ground elder, creeping thistle, docks, dandelions, buttercups, bindweed and couch grass should be removed and burned.

The surface of the site is then covered with a 5 cm (2 in) layer of compost or, if this is not available (as, for example, in a new garden) with a layer of peat, spent hops, leafmould or bark fibre. Some of this layer will be taken down into the subsoil by the action of rain and earthworms so that a yearly topping-up will be needed.

There are certain drawbacks inherent in this system in that, after a limited number of years, the soil fertility of an undug plot appears to deteriorate considerably. Also, the sheer physical effort of making enough compost to keep the plots topped up and barrowing it to the site must be taken into account.

After having drawn attention to the disadvantages, it must be admitted that 'no-digging' gardening can be of value on heavy clay soils where it is well-nigh impossible to maintain a suitably fine surface for the sowing of small seeds by more orthodox methods. The top layer of organic matter created by the 'no-digging' system is valuable not only in the kitchen garden, but also on ornamental beds and borders. Its value is more in question where bedding plants and annuals are concerned, where the regular replacement of plants makes weed control comparatively easy.

Seed sowing

Any discussion of seed sowing brings to mind the proverbial advice to those about to get married – don't! It would be difficult to claim that raising plants from seed is laboursaving, since far less trouble would be involved if you bought them direct from a nurseryman, garden centre or market stall. However, the most economical and enjoyable way of stocking your garden is to grow at least some of the plants from seed, since

Mulching with compost suppresses weeds, conserves moisture and improves the texture and fertility of the soil.

the work is not physically demanding and brings a satisfying sense of achievement.

With the various routine procedures set out below, I have tried to include as many short cuts and labour-saving hints as possible for those who are prepared to 'have a go' at this rewarding task.

Annuals, biennials and perennials (see below for definitions) are all easily propagated from seed. A number of shrubs such as brooms, buddleias, heathers and eucalyptus can also be raised from seed, but it will take several years before they flower or make any real impact in the garden so that it would hardly be worth the effort for the small garden, where only limited numbers of such subjects are needed.

Annuals are plants that grow, flower and set their seed in a single season. Biennials are similar in habit, but do not bloom and make seed until their second season. Both annuals and biennials die off after their life cycle is completed. This is a factor that should be borne in mind if you are a busy gardener. To sidestep the work involved in annual replacements, you may prefer to concentrate on herbaceous perennials, which renew their growth from ground level yearly, or on shrubs, which are the labour-savers *par excellence*.

Both annuals and biennials fall into two categories – hardy and half-hardy. The former can be sown outdoors in spring or early summer and transplanted to their flowering positions as soon as the seedlings are large enough to handle easily. Alternatively, seed can be sown where the plants are to remain, the seedlings being progressively thinned until they are correctly spaced. This saves any transplanting and results in stronger, more vigorous plants. Examples of hardy annuals are annual chrysanthemums, nigella, cornflowers and Virginian stock. Hardy biennials include foxgloves and Canterbury bells.

Half-hardy annuals are normally raised under glass, in heat, during spring and hardened off before being planted out where they are to flower.

Biennials, such as these foxgloves, are sown in late spring or early summer for flowering the following year.

However, from the labour-saving point of view, it is better to sow the seed outdoors, *in situ*, once frost danger is over. Depending on district and season, this is usually in late May or early June. The plants will come into flower some weeks later than those raised in heat, but they are often stronger and more pest and disease resistant. In addition, the work of tending them from the seedling to the flowering stage is much reduced. Half-hardy annuals include antirrhinums (snapdragons), asters, petunias and French marigolds. There are no common half-hardy biennials.

Hardy biennials, and perennials such as wallflowers that are treated as biennials for garden purposes, are sown outdoors in late spring or early summer. The usual procedure is to transplant the seedlings first to a nursery bed before putting them out in their flowering positions in autumn. If you want to cut down on work, however, they can go straight from the seedbed to their permanent situations. They will not be as bushy or vigorous as the twice-transplanted seedlings, so put them closer together than the recommended planting distances. Wallflowers, for

example, should go in with their leaves practically touching, rather than at the normal planting distance of 30 cm (1 ft).

For successful outdoor sowings, you must wait until the soil has warmed up sufficiently in spring to allow the seed to germinate freely and as rapidly as possible. For this, seeds need both warmth and moisture. Sowing too early often means wasted effort, with the seeds germinating irregularly, slowly or not at all. Warming-up of the soil can be speeded up by placing cloches over it. By providing a more even temperature, cloches also cut down the risk of the seedlings suffering from damping-off disease (which is caused by a fungus that attacks the stems of the young plants, causing them to keel over and rot). Cloches are, therefore, time and labour-savers since they cut down on time and trouble spent on growing replacements.

There is no need to break your back when preparing a seedbed. Any weedfree stretch of good garden soil will be suitable, with the surface firmed and raked down to a fine crumbly tilth before the seed is sown.

The depth at which you sow the seed is important, and it will vary

according to the kind of seed and the type and condition of the soil. As a general rule, all seeds should be sown slightly deeper in light soils than in heavy ones. A good general yardstick is to sow the seed twice as deep as its diameter. Nowadays, most seed packets provide much useful information regarding the time and depth at which to sow as well as thinning distances.

Certain hardcoated seeds, such as sweet peas, lupins and broom, will germinate faster if their coats are chipped with a sharp penknife or razor blade. Alternatively, they can be soaked in water for 24 hours before sowing.

In recent years the use of pelleted seed has become increasingly popular, resulting in a considerable saving of time and labour where sowing and thinning are concerned. Only certain kinds of seed are subjected to this process – mainly the very small ones that are difficult both to handle and to sow thinly.

The compound used for the pellets is a type of clay, so that it is essential that the soil in which they are sown is kept moist until germination begins. If, on the other hand, the soil is too wet there is a danger that the pellet-

Cloche types: 1 Reinforced plastic;
2 Perspex high barn; 3 Polythene tunnel;
4 Perspex tent; 5 Corrugated PVC.

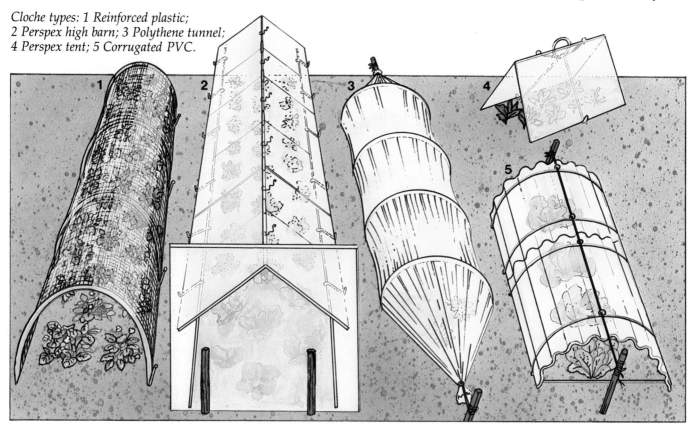

ing material will smother the emerging seedling. Normally, however, it is only on exceptionally heavy wet clay soils that this difficulty is encountered. For really heavy clay soils many gardeners find it worthwhile to line the seed drills with peat or sifted compost. After sowing, water the seedbed lightly, using a watering-can fitted with a fine rose.

Sowing under glass

Given the protection of a greenhouse or cold frame, seeds can be sown under glass in controlled conditions. If you do not possess either of these, a sunny windowsill indoors can be used for the purpose. Seed can be sown in pots, boxes, seed-trays or seed-pans, provided that they are clean and sterile. Containers that have been used previously should be sterilized with a 2% solution of formaldehyde (from gardening shops) or a proprietary product. The containers should stand on a bed of ashes in the greenhouse or frame or on the greenhouse shelving. Pots and seed-pans should have a few broken crocks placed over their drainage holes so that these do not become blocked.

Choose a suitable medium for sowing, such as John Innes No. 1 seed compost or one of the proprietary peat-based seed composts. Boxes can be lined with a thin layer of sphagnum moss.

The compost should be moistened and firmed before the seed is sown and the seed should be covered with a fine layer of sharp sand as a precaution against damping off disease (see page 16). Containers should be covered with a sheet of glass or, where pots are used, they are sealed in a polythene bag until the seed germinates. The bag method is particularly good since there is no need to wipe the condensation off the glass every day.

Much of the time and work taken up by sowing and planting out can be avoided if you sow your seed in pots made of compressed peat. These are filled with a suitable sowing compost and one or two seeds are sown in each. The seedlings can then remain in the pots until it is time for them to be moved to their permanent quarters where they are planted out, still

in the pots. The peat pots disintegrate gradually in the soil, and because of their composition, root growth is encouraged after planting out. Individual peat pots are obtainable for larger seeds such as peas, beans, marrows and sweet peas. For smaller seeds, you can get blocks of small pots that fit into a standard sized tray; these can easily be broken into separate units at planting time.

Equally useful, and more economical after the initial outlay for

Above: A press for DIY soil blocks.

equipment, are the soil blocks that you make yourself with a pot press. The press is filled with moist compost, which is then pushed out on to a seed box or tray in neat 4–5 cm (1½–2 in) cubes. As the roots of the seedlings grow, they bind the soil together, so that the blocks can be planted out at the appropriate time without damaging the delicate roots.

If you have a greenhouse, a propagator can be useful for seeds that are difficult to germinate without artificial heat, saving waste of time and disappointment. It can also be used effectively in a garden room or on a sunny windowsill. The object of a propagator is to provide a correct and even temperature and degree of humidity for seed germination.

As well as simplifying seed-raising, propagators also provide an easy and trouble-free way of increasing stocks of plants from cuttings. Their controlled conditions of temperature and humidity do away with

most of the routine work involved when cuttings are struck under glass in the usual way. By incorporating a thermostat and controlled mist spraying, the entire process can be made almost entirely automatic.

Planting out

Planting out need not be the boring job it is often considered to be. It is one of the most important garden operations and, where trees and shrubs are concerned, the initial planting is like the first down payment on an investment that will declare increasingly valuable dividends for many years to come. This does not mean that you should not take advantage of any methods that will allow you to cut down on the work involved.

Above: This ingenious device speeds up sowing and adjusts for seed size.

Seedlings

Time and disappointment can be saved by planting out seedlings in suitable soil and weather conditions. Ideally, the soil should be moist but not soggy. A good test is to pick up a handful of soil and squeeze it gently; it should retain its shape when pressure is released but break down easily at a touch.

If it can be avoided, seedlings should never be transplanted during long spells of dry weather. Planting out in moist showery conditions will cut down considerably on the time and trouble involved in watering the seedlings to get them established. In any case, artificial watering never does as much good as rain, which creates conditions of atmospheric moisture as well as wetting the soil. It is these conditions, together with warmth, that encourage rapid plant growth and help to ensure success with your seedlings.

The time taken in planting out can also be reduced considerably by using a dibber. This tool consists of a short length of wood, tapered to a point at one end and preferably furnished with a handle at the other, that you push into the soil at appropriate intervals to make the planting holes for the seedlings. You can buy one readymade or make your own from the handle of a worn-out spade or fork. For most types of seedling, a dibber makes a better planting tool than a trowel. All you have to do is drop the seedling into the hole and firm it in with your knuckles.

Bedding plants and perennials

For larger subjects, such as bedding-out plants and perennials, a trowel will be necessary. Get one with a sharp blade, made of stainless steel if possible. Keep it clean when it is not being used. A lot of time can be saved by making the hole and plant-ing in a single operation. You push the blade of the trowel into the soil and press it backwards, dropping the plant into the narrow hole thus formed. Removing the trowel and firming in the plant with your free hand completes the operation. Alternatively, use the blade of the trowel to firm in the plant, as shown in the diagram below. When planting it is essential to plant firmly and avoid leaving any air space.

One useful and labour-saving type of trowel on the market has a self-coiling tape measure recessed into the handle, conveniently to hand for measuring planting distances or easily removable for use elsewhere in the garden. The stainless steel blade also has an embossed depth gauge to simplify planting operations.

Container-grown plants

One of the most revolutionary horticultural developments of the past twenty years or so is the garden centre. This has proved a great stimulus to many people who might otherwise never have taken their gardening seriously. At these garden 'takeaways', container-grown plants are obtainable for putting in at almost any time of the year. Also, instead of having to take plant descriptions on trust from the nurserymen's cata-logues, you can now examine the plants themselves in their full beauty of flower, foliage or berry. By this means, you can achieve the satisfying results of 'instant' gardening.

This mushrooming of garden centres all over the country has inevitably led to the exploitation of the gardening public by a few unscrupulous operators who lack the know-how of the professional nurserymen and are cashing in on the current gardening boom. If you are a newcomer to gardening, it is wise to restrict your garden shopping to reliable nurseries with a proven reputation for quality and expertise.

The most striking development in container-grown plants is among trees and shrubs. Instead of planting being restricted to a few months during their dormant period, it can now be done at any time. This saves labour since it is easier to plant container-grown subjects, you can choose the best planting weather and your planting programme can be spread out over a longer period.

There are, however, certain precautions necessary when planting container-grown plants. Shrubs and conifers must be kept well watered, particularly in dry weather, until their roots have had a chance to establish themselves in their new environment. When evergreens, such

Left: When planting out seedlings, hold the delicate young plants by their leaves (not by their stems or roots, which are much more easily damaged), and firm them in carefully. Below: A dibber is easy to make from an old spade or fork handle and is ideal for planting out seedlings.

as rhododendrons, azaleas, camellias and conifers, are being planted, care must be taken not to break up or disturb the ball of fibrous roots.

Sometimes plants are obtained from the nursery with the roots wrapped up in sacking. If the soil round the roots is intact, cut the string and carefully remove the wrapping. Do not disturb the roots when planting. If the soil round the roots shows signs of crumbling, cut the string and plant the shrub with the sacking intact – this will eventually disintegrate in the soil.

The more carefully the planting holes are prepared, the faster new growth will get going; it is vital to ensure that the hole is both wide and deep enough. A few handfuls of a slow-acting organic fertilizer, such as bonemeal or steamed bone flour, will provide sufficient nourishment for the first few months after planting. Provide a stake if necessary, but always make sure that the soil round the base of the plant is well firmed down so that the plant will not 'rock' in the wind. Frosts can also loosen the soil round plants, even of well established ones, so it pays to check them regularly.

Newly planted container-grown subjects will benefit greatly from a mulch. This will help to retain moisture and cut down on watering. You must remember, however, to rake the mulching material away from the base of the plants when you do water, so that the moisture can penetrate to their roots.

Pruning

Although pruning is an important garden operation, there is no need to make hard work of it or to let it take up too much of your gardening time.

We prune firstly to keep plants within bounds and prevent them from trespassing on their neighbours' living space, and secondly to obtain stronger and better quality growth by directing the energies of the trees or shrubs into a more restricted area of growth. This operation will be much more effective when accompanied by a regular programme of generous feeding.

Another important reason for pruning is to obtain healthy and vigorous plants. In the long run, this

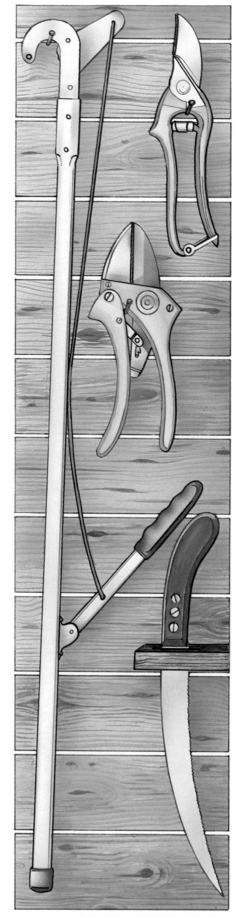

Right: Pruning tools. 1 Long-handled pruners; 2 Parrot-bill secateurs; 3 Anvil secateurs; 4 Curved pruning saw.

is a labour-saving operation. Healthy plants suffer far less from the ravages of pests and diseases, so that you will need to spend less time, trouble and money in combating these.

All dead or diseased growth should be cut out regularly and any inward-growing or crossing stems and branches should also be removed to allow light and air to reach the centre of the plant.

The best secateurs are the 'anvil' and 'parrot-bill' types. The first has one straight cutting blade which cuts onto an anvil of soft metal; the latter has two overlapping curved blades like scissors. Provided that the blades are kept sharpened and in good condition, both will give the sort of clean cut that is desirable. Blunt blades give a ragged cut and this can result in cut branches dying back owing to the entry of disease spores. Parrot-bill blades need expert sharpening; some anvil-type secateurs have replaceable cutting blades.

Long-handled pruners will be needed for pruning trees and tall-growing shrubs. The cutting blades act on a spring and lever principle and they are obtainable with light tubular handles which fit together in sections to give a range of lengths. Older or disabled gardeners will also find these useful for pruning low-growing shrubs without stooping. Another essential tool is a curved pruning saw which enables you to get at awkwardly placed branches.

When large branches are cut off, it is important to paint the entire surface of the wound with an antiseptic dressing, such as Stockholm tar or one of the proprietary wound dressings, to prevent the entry of disease spores.

The tools for the job

As with any other type of gardening equipment, the better the quality, the more easily and efficiently the pruning tools will perform the tasks for which they are intended. There are plenty of cheap secateurs offered for sale, but the blades quickly become blunted and their design often makes them difficult to manipulate.

2·Patios and Lawns

The question facing anyone engaged in creating a new garden or redesigning an existing one is whether to put some of it down to grass and if so, how much; or whether to opt for some kind of more permanent covering – such as bricks, paving or concrete – which, once laid, remains practically trouble-free.

Much will depend on the size of the plot involved and the amount of wear and tear the garden is likely to get. For a really small plot, paving might well be the better choice, especially for gardeners who are also pet lovers or the parents of small children. A paved area adjacent to the house makes a useful place for relaxation, for outdoor meals and barbecues and as a summer parking place for prams and playpens.

Such areas should be sited to the south or west of the house, wherever possible, in order to enjoy the maximum warmth and sunshine. To speak of 'patios' and 'terraces' may sound rather pretentious but don't let this deter you, however small your garden may be. One of the most attractive 'gardens' I have ever seen was little more than a small backyard, only a few metres in area. It adjoined an old house in Chichester and had been transformed by its owner into a perfect place for relaxation by the skilful blending of old paving slabs, wall shrubs and climbing plants plus the careful positioning of two stone plant containers and a bird bath of classic design. This, indeed, was the labour-saving garden *par excellence*.

A well-planned, easily cared for patio.

Paving

Provided that the work of laying it is properly carried out, paving should prove to be practically trouble-free. There are many different kinds of material to choose from, ranging from natural stone slabs through various types of man-made materials to crazy paving.

Although the use of crazy paving has often been sneered at, there is a great deal to be said for it, provided that the broken stone of which it is constructed is natural and also that it is properly laid. It is those bits of broken concrete or synthetic paving, or stretches of concrete marked out in a random pattern that have given crazy paving its bad reputation. Properly laid random paving can look perfect in a country setting, although it is usually out of place in towns or in association with modern architecture.

For contemporary houses, the best choice would be either slabs of artificial stone paving, obtainable in a variety of sizes and colours; bricks or pebbles set in concrete; or a combination of two or more of these.

York stone slabs, which used to be easily available, are now in short supply and expensive. Although their colour and texture enhance the beauty of paths and terraces, York slabs also have their drawbacks since they can vary considerably in thickness, making it difficult to obtain a level surface. However, since there are now so many attractive paving slabs of artificial stone, including some with the ripples and weathered look of York, and others which give the appearance of granite setts, most gardeners can find an acceptable alternative.

The slabs come in a variety of shapes and sizes, but those that are 45 cm (18 in) square or less are the best, since they are easiest to handle. I prefer either natural grey or sand-coloured slabs: white produces terrible glare in summer, while the brighter colours, such as reds and greens, are more suited to swimming pools and seaside promenades.

Laying paving can be hard work, and if you are not prepared for this, you should enlist outside help. However, if you decide to save a good deal of money rather than time, there is the enormous satisfaction of doing it yourself. The easiest way of laying paving slabs is to put them directly on to the soil. This, however, requires a light sandy soil and a comparatively level site. It is not easy to get a good level on heavy clay soils, and uneven levels can cause shifting and even cracking of the slabs. On such soils, the slabs can be laid on a firm bed of sand, which saves the effort and expense of using a cement

mix as a foundation.

These methods are suitable only for paths and patios over which there will not be a great deal of traffic.

For more permanent paving, the site should be levelled and a layer of rubble, 10–15 cm (4–6 in) deep, spread over the surface and rammed down. On top of this, a 5 cm (2 in) layer of coarse sand should be spread out, trodden down and raked level. The paving slabs can then be laid directly onto this sand bed. Each slab should be tapped down, making sure that the correct level is maintained as laying proceeds. Individual slabs can be tested with a spirit level, but for the overall surface a straight edge or levelling board will be needed.

When paths or patios are laid dry, you must be prepared for a certain amount of movement. This can be due to various causes – for example, the leaching of the sand base after heavy rain or the burrowing activities of mice or moles. For areas in constant use, it is better to lay the slabs in a wet concrete mixture – 1 part of cement to 6 of sand – 10 cm (4 in) deep.

A lot of the hard work involved can be avoided by using ready-mixed concrete, but make sure the site is ready when this is delivered. Guard, too, against concrete burns by protecting your hands with gloves.

The paving slabs are laid on the wet surface of the concrete after it has been tamped down with the edge of a board and levelled off with a straight-edge and spirit level. Do not lay the paving above the level of the house damp course and make sure that any paved area next to the house has a gentle slope away from it to allow rainwater to drain away.

Where a large area of paving is being laid, variety will add interest to an unbroken expanse of slabs. This can be achieved in several ways – by interlaying small stretches of slabs of a different colour, by leaving planting holes in which small shrubs, bulbs or bedding plants can be grown, or by filling squares or rectangles with materials of contrasting appearance such as pebbles, bricks or flints. Omitting slabs at intervals where walls and paving meet will make room for planting climbers and wall shrubs.

Inexperienced gardeners or those with very little time to spare may prefer to turn over the work described above to a professional or part-time workman. It must be re-

Patio

- Patio provides an attractive, easy-care recreation area between house and garden.
- Well-laid anti-slip paving stones are gently sloped to ensure rainwater drains *away* from house.
- All the plants require the minimum amount of care and attention.
- The culinary herbs are within easy reach of the kitchen.
- The shrubs will eventually hide the fence and need the minimum of pruning.
- All the herbaceous plants have easy-care qualities: should not need staking and will not need dividing or transplanting for many years.
- Creeping and trailing plants 'break up' the paved area yet need minimal attention.

Key:
1. *Wisteria sinensis*
2. *Yucca filamentosa*
3. *Clematis jackmanii*
4. *Lysimachia nummularia* (Creeping Jenny)
5. *Calluna vulgaris*
6. Pyracantha 'Orange Glow' (Firethorn)
7. *Choisya ternata* (Mexican Orange Blossom)
8. *Juniperus x media*
9. *Chaenomeles speciosa* 'Rowallane Seedling' (Japonica)
10. *Hedera colchica dentata* 'Variegata' (Giant Ivy)
11. *Oxalis inops* (Wood Sorrel)
12. Lobelia
13. *Chamaecyparis lawsoniana* 'Nana' (Dwarf Cypress)
14. *Alyssum saxatile*
15. Aubrieta
16. *Iberis sempervirens* (Perennial Candytuft)
17. Herbs — Sage, Thyme, Tarragon, Parsley, Marjoram
18. Hosta 'Thomas Hogg' (Plaintain Lily)
19. *Thymus serpyllum coccineus* (Creeping Thyme)
20. *Acanthus spinosus*
21. Bergenia 'Ballawley Hybrid'
22. *Phormium tenax* (New Zealand Flax)

Left: Creeping plants relieve the bareness of walls and paving on this patio. Right: A silver birch makes a central feature for this spacious lawn.

fine crumb-like texture. About a week before sowing the seed, or turfing, a dressing of lawn fertilizer should be raked into the surface soil at the rate of $60 \, g/m^2$ (2 oz/sq yd).

Lawns from seed

This is a cheaper way of making a lawn than by turfing and should also result in a better, more weed-free lawn. The main disadvantage of making lawns from seed is the additional work involved in preparation and the longer waiting time before the grass is fit for use. Set against this, however, is the fact that you can select a seed without coarse grasses, which will produce a lawn that will need a lot less time spent on maintenance and cutting than one made from turf. A seed mixture containing rye grass would, however, be a better choice where the lawn is likely to be subjected to a good deal of wear and tear; such a mixture is cheaper than one containing fine grasses only.

Grass seed can be sown either in spring or autumn. Autumn sowings save labour as the soil is warm, germination is more rapid and there is less likelihood of birds eating the seed. Spring-sown lawns have to face the hazards of long spells of dry weather, and regular watering will be needed in the initial stages. In spring, food for the birds is in short supply and they may eat much of the seed unless you protect the site with netting. However, it is possible to buy seed that has been treated with a chemical that makes it unpalatable to some seed-eating birds (the treated seed is harmless to humans, birds and other animals).

Sow the seed at the rate of 45–60 g/m^2 (1½–2 oz/sq yd), and to ensure even distribution, divide the seed into two equal lots, sowing one batch in one direction and the other in a direction at right angles to the first. A light raking will be enough to cover the seed. Germination should take about 15 days in spring and a week in autumn. The first cut can be given when the grass is 5 cm (2 in) tall, with the blades of the mower set high.

membered, however, that the labour involved is a once-and-for-all project that is going to save hours of work in the long run.

Lawns

The quality of a lawn depends, to a great extent, on the amount of work put into its initial preparation and subsequent maintenance. Such preparation is important whether a new lawn is being made from seed or turf. There is no need to dig over the site to a great depth unless the builders, as is so often the case, have spread the infertile subsoil from the foundations over the prospective lawn area. Otherwise, a light forking over should be sufficient. You should remove all perennial weeds, such as

dandelions, ground elder and bindweed, as this operation progresses; annual weeds can be buried so that they will rot down to humus.

When you have forked over the entire site for the lawn, you should give the surface soil an initial raking. Break down large clods of earth by treading or by pulling a light roller over them when the soil is comparatively dry. During the raking process, remove any large stones and level out all bumps and hollows. If your garden is on a slope, don't worry too much about getting the site dead level. You will save a great deal of time and trouble if you aim instead at a properly graded slope that follows the natural contours of the land.

Tread and rake the entire surface several times until it is firm and of a

Lawns from turf

Making a lawn from turf involves less work than making one from seed. The preparation of the surface need not be as thorough and turf can be laid at almost any time of year. Turves are of standard size and uniform thickness. They measure 1 m ×30 cm (3×1 ft) and are approximately 4 cm (1½ in) thick. The best turf is the so-called Cumberland variety, but this is not for the busy gardener. Cumberland turf needs a site prepared by an expert, great care in laying and endless attention once established.

Parkland turf, if you can get it, will make a fine lawn. Failing this, downland turf, in which the finer grasses predominate, will be quite satisfactory. With regular mowing and fertilizing, these finer grasses can be encouraged at the expense of the coarser varieties. Turf can sometimes be obtained from local builders or nurseries; failing this, go to a specialist turf supplier (see Yellow Pages).

Lay the turves as soon as possible after delivery. If you have to delay this job for more than a few days, you should lay the turves out flat and water them in dry weather.

Begin turfing at one corner of the site and, after you have laid the first row, use a board to stand on to lay subsequent rows, to protect the turf. Never stand on the prepared soil surface, as this is liable to make hollows, resulting in an uneven surface when the lawn is finished. Lay the turves like bricks in a wall, with the joints staggered in adjacent rows. Never lay small pieces of turf at the edges of the lawn. If you cannot complete a row using whole pieces only lay a whole turf at the edge and use the pieces inside.

When you have finished laying, fill in the joints between the turves by brushing in a mixture of sifted soil and sand. Autumn-laid turf will not usually need its first cut until the following spring. Make the first few cuts with the mower blades set high, gradually reducing the height to about 1.2 cm (½ in). Cutting too closely is not the time-saver it might seem to be; it makes for a lot of unnecessary work later by creating bald patches in which weeds will gain a foothold.

If you are starting from scratch on a new plot of former pastureland, it is often possible to transform this into a passable lawn, provided that the site is reasonably level. Such lawns, however, will need more frequent cutting and attention to weed control. In the long run, therefore, you will usually save labour by making your new lawn from seed or turf.

Edging

A well-kept edge greatly enhances the appearance of any lawn, but edging can be a time-consuming chore. There are two alternatives for the labour-saving garden. Special metal strips can be bought, or a narrow row of paving stones can be laid along the edge. Either method will help to keep the grass from encroaching on adjacent beds and, at the same time, prevent edging plants from spilling over onto the lawn.

Tools and equipment

The choice of tools and equipment for the lawn depends largely on the area of grass involved. Even for the pocket handkerchief plot, however, you can buy a small, powered rotary mower that will take the backache out of grass cutting and keep the lawn in tiptop condition. Such small power mowers are usually mains-operated. Models with more conventional cutting blades are also obtainable, powered by batteries.

Large petrol-engined rotary and hover mowers are useful labour-savers where larger areas of grass are concerned (up to ⅓ or ½ an acre). The former kind are now usually obtainable with a grass-collecting box – a worthwhile labour-saving extra. The ultimate in labour-saving luxury is a sit-on powered mower, but these are only a practical investment for really large lawns.

There are many kinds of sprinkler for every size of lawn. The travelling kind, that you can turn on and forget for several hours, is the easiest to operate but less sophisticated kinds would be more suitable for small lawns. However, it is very important to conserve water supplies, and your local authority may well impose a 'no-hose' ban in dry summers. There is no need, however, to break your back carrying cans of water for the parched grass. Your lawn may turn brown and look a sorry sight, but grass is exceptionally resilient, and even after the near desert conditions of the summer of '76, most lawns made miraculous recoveries once the dry spell was over.

Spreaders of various kinds, both hand-held and wheeled, are useful for the application of fertilizers and weedkillers. Another useful tool is a wire-tined rake for scarifying the lawn before the first cut in spring to remove dead grass, moss and clover.

Metal edging strips or paving slabs cut down the work of lawn edge trimming.

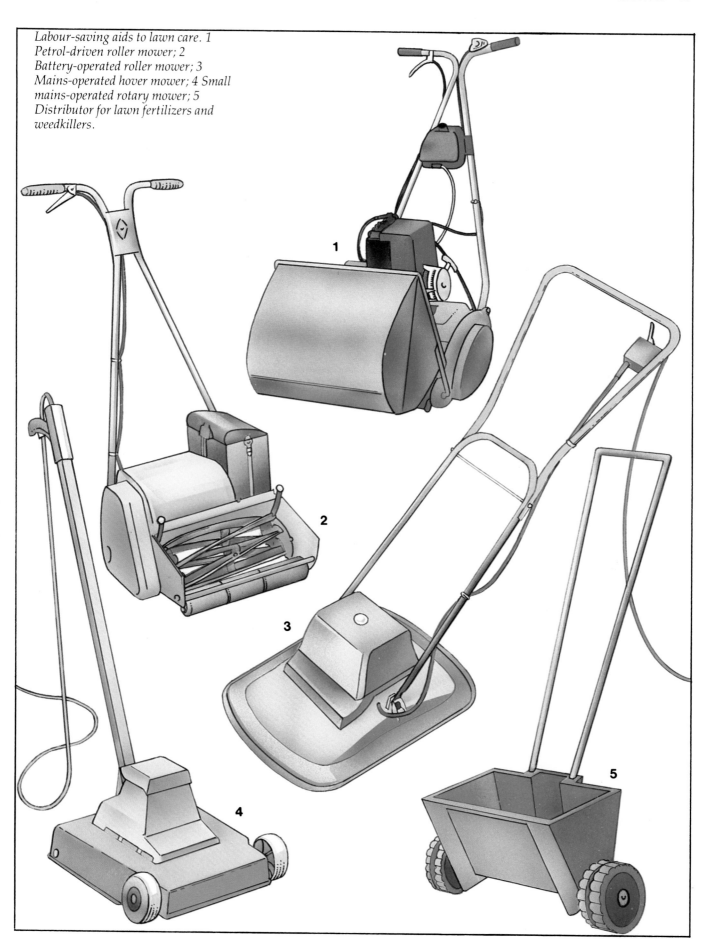

Labour-saving aids to lawn care. 1 Petrol-driven roller mower; 2 Battery-operated roller mower; 3 Mains-operated hover mower; 4 Small mains-operated rotary mower; 5 Distributor for lawn fertilizers and weedkillers.

Weeding and feeding programmes

Like any other plant, grass needs its fair share of nourishment if it is to remain vigorous and healthy. Weeds will rob the grasses of food and living space, and if they are not controlled they will soon make a takeover bid for large patches of the lawn. Treating weeds regularly, before they have had time to take a firm hold, will save much time and labour later.

The two operations of weeding and feeding go together to a large extent. Programmes of weed control should always be accompanied by applications of a suitable lawn fertilizer to stimulate the growth of the grass. It will then quickly fill in any bare patches left by the dead weeds.

Many brands of selective lawn weedkillers do, in fact, incorporate a fertilizer so that the two operations can be carried out at the same time. When the young grasses first appear, a number of weed seedlings are likely to come up at the same time. A large proportion of them will be annual weeds, which can be removed easily by hand. More stubborn are the perennial weeds, such as docks, dandelions, daisies and plantains. Some can be removed by hand, but many will have to remain until the new grass is established, usually after about six months, before selective weedkillers can be applied. The three weedkillers in common use, marketed under different brand names, are 2,4-d, MCPA and mecoprop. The latter is used to treat clover, against which the other two are not effective. Applications can be made at any time during the growing season, but they are most effective when the weeds are growing vigorously during early summer.

Spraying is generally considered to be the most efficient way of applying weedkillers, but for ease and safety of application I prefer to use those in powder form. These usually incorporate a lawn fertilizer and often a colourant as well, which enables you to see the areas you have treated and so prevents over or under-doses. Where lawn weeds are not too prevalent, it is a waste of time and trouble to give the lawn an overall treatment.

Spot applicators are available for this purpose, as well as a 'cane' that injects a lethal dose of weedkiller into the roots of individual weeds.

When using selective hormone weedkillers, always remember that they are fatal to many types of garden plants. Choose, therefore, a still day for spraying or dusting and watch out for drift onto adjacent beds and borders. Remember, too that most weedkillers are toxic to man and animals, so keep small children and pets away from an immediately treated area and keep all weedkillers in their original containers in a securely locked cupboard out of reach of children. Wash your hands thor-

A well-maintained and healthy lawn.

oughly after using weedkillers. Do not use the mowings from treated lawns as a mulch or on a compost heap. For an environmentally safer and cheaper alternative, use lawn sand – buy it ready-mixed from a garden shop, or mix thoroughly 3 parts (by weight) of sulphate of ammonia, 1 part sulphate of iron and 20 parts sharp (lime-free) sand. Apply during spring and summer at 120 g per m² (4 oz per sq yd) during dry weather; a good pinch sprinkled onto individual dandelions, plantains or other troublesome weeds will kill them individually. Lawn sand feeds the grass as well as killing the weeds. Mowings can be safely used on the compost heap and as a mulch.

Badly-drained or moss-infested lawns can be improved by a dressing of sharp sand or coke breeze in autumn. This will give the soil structure a more open texture and allows any moisture to drain away more easily. Autumn, too, is the time to feed the lawn with a top dressing of peat or well-rotted manure or compost. This will build up a fertile layer just below the surface, where the grass roots can take full advantage of it, and especially where new lawns are concerned, help to fill any surface irregularities that may have developed.

Moss can be eradicated by treating affected patches of lawn with lawn sand at the rate given above or with a proprietary liquid moss killer based on a tar product, anthracene. Unless the basic cause is found, however, the mosses are likely to reappear. Many different factors are responsible, including poor or waterlogged soil, too acid a soil or too close cutting of the grass. It is better therefore to save unnecessary work by finding the cause and putting matters right before resorting to preventive measures.

Lawn maintenance may sound a formidable task, but unless you are a perfectionist whose aim is to have a lawn like a bowling green, you can cut down on some of the routine jobs and still have a stretch of grass that will make a pleasing setting for your plants and a place for relaxation. In any case, the work involved decreases considerably once you have got the lawn into condition. Also, many of the maintenance operations usually recommended, such as top-

dressing, scarifying and spiking, can be dispensed with by the busy gardener.

Renovating old lawns

On taking over a garden where the lawn has been badly neglected, one's first impulse might be to dig up the whole area and start again at square one. This entails a lot of hard work and is not necessarily the best procedure unless the turf has become infested with coarse grasses, moss and weeds to the point of no return. In many cases a great deal of labour can be saved by renovating the existing lawn.

Sickling down the tall growth will give a better idea of the situation. After that, a thorough raking will get rid of the inevitable accumulation of dead material. The grass should then be cut with the mower, with the blades set at their highest level. A rotary mower is ideal for this job.

Patience will bring satisfying results, as the finer grasses regain light and air and begin to multiply. If a renovation programme of this kind is started in spring, combined with applications of lawn fertilizers and weedkiller, good results should be produced by the following autumn. At this stage, bare patches can be filled with seed mixed with sifted soil or peat, or can be made good by patching with turf. Subsequent maintenance will be the same as for an established lawn.

Pests

The only lawn pest likely to prove troublesome in most gardens is the leatherjacket, a greyish-black leathery grub, the larva of the cranefly, or daddylonglegs. These feed on the grass roots, and although they often do no lasting damage, in some years they can cause a lot of harm and kill off large areas of grass, particularly if the lawn is newly sown. They can, however, be easily controlled by soaking the infested areas with water and then covering with sacking or black polythene sheeting. This should bring the leatherjackets to the surface by the following morning, when the covers can be removed and the grubs swept up and destroyed or left for the birds to eat.

3·Ground Cover Plants

One of the most effective and labour-saving ways of controlling weeds is by means of ground cover plants. They are particularly useful for this purpose as an underplanting to roses and other shrubs, in borders and on sloping banks. They require little or no maintenance beyond the occasional cutting back of the more rampant types.

You cannot expect ground cover plants to smother established perennial weeds. For this reason, it is most important to prepare the ground as thoroughly as possible before planting, forking over the soil and removing all perennial weeds and their roots. This job will be amply repaid by the reduction in the need for weeding later. On poor soils, or in old, neglected gardens, it is a good idea to add manure, compost or fertilizer to the soil to get the plants off to a good start.

The time taken for ground cover plants to establish a weed-smothering carpet will vary according to the subject chosen. Most of those listed below will be doing their appointed job by the end of their second season. Some, like the Variegated Deadnettle, will have made a dense overall carpet by the end of their first season. Until this happens, normal weeding of annual weeds must be carried out.

Using ground cover plants cannot work instant miracles, but it can eventually cut down the task of weeding to negligible proportions. The list shows the situations in which the various plants will thrive, but for

Rose of Sharon, Hypericum calycinum.

dense shade under trees I would recommend one of the vigorous spreading shrubs such as the Rose of Sharon, *Hypericum calycinum*, or the Snowberry, *Symphoricarpos albus*.

In the rock garden you could use creeping perennials of mat-like growth to keep areas free from weeds. Choose for this purpose the less vigorous and invasive kinds of ground cover plants to avoid a complete takeover of the choicer alpines. The smaller polygonums, the lungworts, and the colourful rock phlox and rock pinks are all ideal for this purpose.

Alphabetical List of Ground Cover Plants

The figures immediately after the name of each plant give its approximate height and spread after 2 to 3 seasons.

Key to abbreviations:	
D – Deciduous	P – Perennial
E – Evergreen	S – Shrub

Ajuga reptans
Bugle (DP)
10×90 cm (4 in×3 ft)
These are low-growing plants with a rapid rate of spread, closely related to our native wild bugle. They bear upright spikes of gentian blue flowers in late spring. 'Atropurpurea', with handsome coppery coloured foliage, is the most vigorous form. 'Variegata', with cream and grey-green leaves, and 'Tricolor', whose copper and purple leaves are blotched with

Above: Lady's Mantle, Alchemilla mollis. *Left:* Cotoneaster salicifolius.

cream, are less rampant and suitable for the rock garden.
Soil – any
Sun or shade

Alchemilla mollis
Lady's Mantle (DP)
60×30 cm (2×1 ft)
This is a plant of great beauty with attractive silken-textured, rounded pale green leaves and dainty sprays of lime-green flowers much prized by arrangers. *Alchemilla* associates particularly well with roses. It spreads rapidly by means of self-sown seed.
Soil – any
Sun

Anaphalis triplinervis (DP)
30×30 cm (1×1 ft)
This is a silver-leaved herbaceous plant that forms dense spreading mats, bearing clusters of small white 'everlasting' flowers in late summer.
Soil – any
Sun

Bergenia (EP)
30×60 cm (1×2 ft)
Formerly known as megaseas, these

members of the saxifrage family have large rounded or spoon-shaped evergreen leaves. In some forms, these turn a vivid crimson colour in winter. Cultivars such as 'Ballawley Hybrid' (also known as 'Delbees'), with magenta flowers; 'Evening Glow', with rose-red flowers; and 'Silver Light' ('Silberlicht'), with white flowers, are all superior to the type.
Soil – any
Sun or part shade

Calluna
See Heathers

Cotoneaster (ES)
Various heights and spreads
Several of the cotoneaster species are of a prostrate creeping habit, covering the ground with a dense mat of leaves and wiry stems. Among the best of this type are *C. adpressus*, a dwarf spreading shrub with scarlet fruits and crimson autumn foliage; *C. dammeri*, with longer trailing stems and masses of red berries in autumn and early winter; and *C. microphyllus*, a dwarf small-leaved shrub with larger red fruits than most other kinds. Two more, useful for covering banks or old tree stumps, are the Fishbone Cotoneaster, *C. horizontalis*, so named because of the herringbone structure of its branches, and *C. salicifolius*, the Willow-leaved Cotoneaster. Both of these carry abundant crops of small scarlet berries from autumn until the New Year. The leaves of the former variety turn a brilliant shade of red in autumn.
Soil – any
Sun or part shade

Epimedium
Barrenwort (DP)
30×30 cm (1×1 ft)
The barrenworts, with their preference for light shade, make attractive ground cover underneath rhododendrons and other shade-tolerant shrubs. The dainty sprays of minute columbine-type flowers add to the attraction of their delicate foliage in early spring. 'Rose Queen' has its leaves tinged with copper, and rosy-purple flowers.
Soil – any
Part shade

Erica
See Heathers

Bell Heather, Erica cinerea.

Euonymus fortunei
Trailing plant (ES)
This attractive evergreen shrub is a relative of our native spindle tree. The variety *radicans* is the one most widely grown as ground cover. Good named cultivars include 'Silver Queen', whose leaves are edged with white, and 'Variegatus', with grey-green leaves margined with white and tinged with pink. All of these are useful plants for chalk soils.
Soil – any, including chalk
Sun or part shade

Heathers
Erica and *Calluna* (ES)
Various heights and spreads
There can be few more effective or decorative ground cover plants than the cultivated forms of heather and ling. Once they are established, usually by their third season, none but the most persistent weeds can find a foothold under their dense mat of wiry stems and close carpet of foliage.

Heathers, too are among the most useful garden all-rounders. By choosing suitable species and varieties, you can have a display of flowers in every month of the year, including December and January. Nothing paints a more colourful garden picture in winter than the Winter Heath, *Erica carnea*, which blooms from January to March. In summer, a similar effect is obtained from our native Ling, *Calluna vulgaris*, the Dorset Heath, *E. ciliaris* and the Bell Heather, *E. cinerea*, which will provide a display lasting from June to November. The gap between autumn and winter can be bridged by early-flowering cultivars of *E. carnea*, such as 'Eileen Porter' and 'Winter Beauty'.

Heathers do best in a sunny situation and light, well-drained soils. Heavier soils should be lightened by the addition of quantities of peat or leafmould. Heathers should be planted 40–60 cm (15–24 in) apart to form a continuous carpet. They look most effective planted in groups of three or more of a kind.

Most of the summer-flowering heathers are lime-haters and need a slightly acid soil. Of them, only the Cornish Heath, *Erica vagans*, is tolerant of lime. The Winter Heath, *E. carnea*, will tolerate a moderately alkaline soil and would be the best choice for most gardens. Varieties grown for their coloured foliage, such as 'Golden Drop' or 'Aurea', must have a position in full sun if the colouring is to develop to the full.

SUMMER-FLOWERING HEATHS Lime tolerant: *Erica vagans* cultivars: 'Diana Hornibrook' with coral-pink flowers; 'Mrs. D. F. Maxwell', pink; and 'St. Keverne', lilac pink. Lime haters: *Calluna vulgaris* cultivars: 'H. E. Beale', silver-pink; 'Peter Sparks', pink; 'Ruth Sparks', white, all with double flowers. *Erica cinerea* cultivars; 'Alba', white; 'Anne Berry', with pink flowers and golden foliage; 'C. D. Eason', vivid crimson.

WINTER-FLOWERING HEATHS (all lime tolerant) *Erica carnea* cultivars: 'James Backhouse', pale pink; 'Ruby Glow', rosy crimson; 'Springwood Pink' and 'Springwood White'; 'Vivelli', deep crimson with copper foliage; and 'December Red', deep rose-pink. *Erica darleyensis* cultivars: 'Arthur Johnson', magenta; 'W. T. Ratcliffe', white with dark green foliage.
Soil – see above
Sun

Hedera
Ivy (ES)
Various spreads
Normally, we think of ivies as climbing plants but many of them perform an equally useful function as ground cover plants. They form dense, weed-suppressing mats and are particularly useful for shady beds.

One of the best and most vigorous kinds is the Common Ivy, *Hedera helix*, in its many varied forms. Some of the showier cultivars are 'Buttercup', with golden foliage; 'Glacier', whose leaves are silver-grey, edged with white; 'Goldheart', a striking ivy whose emerald green leaves are splashed with yellow; and 'Tricolor', whose grey-green and white leaves take on a pink flush in winter.

H. colchica, the Persian Ivy, has much larger leaves than those of *H. helix*. They measure up to 20 cm (8 in) in length in some forms. This species, too, includes cultivars with strikingly variegated leaves, such as 'Dentata Variegata', with bright green and cream foliage, and 'Paddy's Pride', which has deep green leaves beautifully marked with bold yellow.
Soil – any
Sun or shade

Helianthemum
Sun Rose (ES)
20×60 cm (8 in×2 ft)
The sun roses (sometimes misnamed 'rock roses') make first-class cover for the rock garden or for the fronts of beds and borders. Their low, trailing growth will soon carpet large areas. The plants are covered in bloom over a long period during early summer. After they have finished flowering, sun roses should be lightly trimmed with a pair of shears. Some of the best kinds for ground cover are 'Ben Hope', with orange-red flowers; 'Ben More', orange; 'Rhodanthe Carneum', pink; 'St. John's College', yellow; and 'The Bride', which has cream-white flowers with yellow centres.
Soil – light, well drained
Sun

Hosta
Plantain Lily (DP)
Various heights and spreads
Hostas are handsome foliage plants with broad, deeply-ribbed, plantain-like leaves and attractive white or pale mauve flower spikes that appear around midsummer. Their dense clumps of foliage will keep all kinds of weed in check. Among the best forms are *H. albomarginata*, which has pale green leaves edged with cream; 'Thomas Hogg', one of the best named cultivars and similar to the former variety; *H. crispula*, whose fluted dark green leaves are margined with cream; and *H. sieboldiana*, a magnificent plant, with leaves as much as 60 cm (2 ft) long and 30 cm (1 ft) in width and of a blue-green colour. The latter is sometimes referred to as *H. glauca*.
Soil – fairly moist
Sun or part shade

Hypericum calycinum
Rose of Sharon (ES)
30 cm (1 ft), spreading
This dwarf evergreen member of the St. John's Wort family is one of the finest ground cover plants for dense shade and poor soils. It makes an ideal choice for clothing shady banks and similar situations where few other plants can be grown successfully. The golden flowers, each with its central boss of stamens, resemble those of a single-flowered rose and are open during June and July. The

Rose of Sharon increases rapidly by means of underground suckers and will soon cover a large area.
Soil – any
Sun or shade

Lamium
Cultivated Deadnettle (DP)
30 cm (1 ft), spreading
There are several garden forms of the wild deadnettle that make effective ground cover plants. The most rampant is *Lamium galeobdolon* 'Variegatum', whose leaves are attractively mottled with silver to provide a telling contrast to the whorls of yellow flowers in spring. This species increases rapidly by underground runners and will thrive even in dense shade. *L. maculatum* is much less vigorous but will perform its cover-up job well in the front of the border. The leaves are dark green with a white stripe and the flowers are purple. There is also a golden-leaved form, 'Aureum', but this is less vigorous than the type.
Soil – any
Sun or shade

Pachysandra terminalis
Japanese Spurge (ES)
20 cm (8 in), spreading
This is a dwarf evergreen shrub that provides excellent ground cover in moist shady situations. The thick lobed leaves are borne in rosettes at the end of the stems, and the greenish-white flowers appear in early spring. 'Variegata', with white-variegated leaves, is less rampant than the type.
Soil – any except chalk
Moist shade

Polygonum
Bistort (DP)
Various heights and spreads
Several of the bistorts provide first-rate ground cover, although some are too vigorous for the average-sized garden. Two of the more restrained forms, which both form dense mats of weed-smothering foliage, are *Polygonum affine* 'Darjeeling Red', with small crimson flower spikes and leaves that turn bronze in autumn; and *P. bistorta superba*, a taller variety with pink flower spikes borne on tall stems from late summer to autumn.
Soil – any
Sun

Santolina
Cotton Lavender (ES)
45×30 cm (1½×1 ft)
These 'evergrey' dwarf shrubs, with their finely cut, silvery foliage and yellow button flowers at midsummer, make attractive ground cover for the edge of a mixed border. The two best species for this purpose are *Santolina chamaecyparissus* and *S. neapolitana.* 'Nana' is a delightful dwarf cultivar of the former species; 'Edward Bowles' is the best form of the latter.
Soil – light, well drained
Sun

Saxifraga umbrosa
London Pride (EP)
20×20 cm (8×8 in)
An old cottage-garden favourite which is easy to grow and has a rapid rate of spread. It is useful in shady borders and will flourish in the

Hostas are excellent ground cover plants. This is Hosta albomarginata.

poorest soils. Close-packed rosettes of dark green leathery leaves set off the dainty sprays of pale pink flowers, which appear in early summer.
Soil – any
Sun or shade

Symphoricarpos
Snowberry (DS)
1.5 m (5 ft)
The snowberries are vigorous suckering shrubs, some of which are too rampant for the average garden. They all bear decorative white or pinkish berries that persist through the winter, since the birds leave them alone.
  Symphoricarpos albus laevigatus is the Common Snowberry, with white mothball berries, ideal as cover under the dense shade of trees. More attractive and less vigorous are cultivars such as 'Magic Berry' and 'Mother of Pearl', both of which have rose pink berries.
Soil – any
Sun or shade

Symphytum
Comfrey (DP)
45×60 cm (1½×3 ft)
There are several species of comfrey, the best of which for rapid spread and dense cover is *Symphytum grandiflorum*. This species bears clusters of creamy-yellow flowers, edged with red at the bud stage, over a long period from spring to midsummer.
Soil – any
Moist shade

Tiarella
Foam Flower (DP)
30 cm (1 ft), spreading
An attractive, low-growing, creeping perennial, which bears masses of feathery white flower spikes in early summer. *Tiarella cordifolia* is the more vigorous species; *T. wherryi* can be distinguished from the former by the pinkish tinge to its flowers. The mat-forming leaves are heart-shaped and of a soft green colour.
Soil – any
Partial shade

4 · Conifers and Hedging

Conifers provide a fast and easy answer to many of the problems of cutting down on maintenance work. Their great variety of form, size and habit makes them suitable for gardens of any size, from the pocket-handkerchief plot upwards.

The best choices for the smaller garden are found among the cypresses, junipers, pines and thuyas. If you have a good deal of space, however, you may well be able to find room for larch, cedar, fir or spruce, which will grow into tall, stately trees. Choose your planting site carefully: when they are mature, these trees will cast a lot of shade.

In addition to serving as valuable specimen plants in lawns or borders, where they will give trouble-free service for a lifetime, numerous species and varieties of conifer make ideal hedging material.

Most conifers are tolerant of a wide range of soil conditions and many will thrive in partial shade. Few of them, however, will tolerate drastic cutting back, so it pays to choose carefully, particularly if they are to be used in important focal positions when it is better to let them develop their own typical shapes and outlines.

Once planted, specimen conifers need only minimal attention which consists mainly of keeping the soil at their base free from weeds for the first few seasons. After this, the dense carpet of needles and the shade which they cast will suppress all weed growth.

For a trouble-free border, a selection of conifers and shrubs is hard to beat.

One of the best garden conifers is the popular Lawson's Cypress, *Chamaecyparis lawsoniana*. As well as making a handsome specimen tree, it is also useful for hedging, as it can be clipped neatly up to a height of 3 m (10 ft) or more. Of the many fine cultivars, 'Allumii' makes a sturdy blue-green column; 'Columnaris' is slimmer in outline, with closely packed, bright green foliage. There are several attractive forms with golden foliage, including 'Golden King', with drooping branches, 'Golden Wonder', of more upright habit, and 'Lanei' which makes a neat golden-yellow pyramid.

The junipers, with their many and varied shapes and habits, are almost as popular as the cypresses. They are the best choice of conifer if you garden on chalk, although they do just as well on most other types of soil. The Irish Juniper, *Juniperus communis* 'Hibernica', is the kind most widely planted. Its pencil-slim column makes it an ideal choice to use as a specimen tree for a formal garden or patio. The Irish Juniper is particularly useful in the smaller garden since it will seldom grow more than 3 m (10 ft) tall.

J. pfitzeriana, the 'Pfitzer Juniper', is also noteworthy for its moderate size and slow rate of growth. Its habit is wide and spreading and it is adaptable to most soils and situations, thriving even under the shade of deciduous trees. There are several interesting forms, including 'Aurea', whose foliage is tipped with gold when the new growth appears in summer, 'Plumosa' with green feathery foliage, and 'Plumosa Aurea'

with striking golden leaves.

J. sabina is another good choice for gardens of small to medium size. There are various cultivars, including 'Hicksii', with grey-blue leaves, *tamariscifolia*, which makes a flat-topped bush of feathery foliage, and 'Cupressifolia', with long horizontal branches seldom more than 6 cm (2½ in) above ground level. The low spreading branches make 'Cupressifolia' ideal for a patio, because they relieve the monotony of stretches of paving without obscuring the view.

We do not normally think of yews as specimen conifers but usually as hedging plants. There are, however, several attractive forms that make good garden specimens. *Taxus baccata fastigiata*, the Irish Yew, is one of these. It makes a dense, dark green column, which may be rather sepulchral for some tastes. The golden form 'Aureomarginata' has a more cheerful appearance, similar in habit but with leaves that are tipped with gold. There are also dwarf and prostrate yews that are useful in the rock or heath garden or for clothing shady banks. 'Nana' and 'Cavendishii', both less than 1 m (3 ft) in height, are good examples of these.

Hedging

For a garden, a hedge is the living equivalent of a frame for a picture. It enhances the beauty of what is inside it, as well as acting as a valuable windbreak and a screen to give privacy. The choice of hedging material is very wide, and needs careful consideration if you are to cut down on maintenance as much as possible.

As already mentioned, conifers are widely used nowadays, even in the smallest gardens, as hedging plants. In this capacity they are first-rate labour-savers and normally need clipping only once a year, in late summer. This compares favourably with the requirements of some other hedging shrubs, such as privet and lonicera, which are in constant need of attention in summer and autumn.

For a rapid and dense evergreen screen, there is nothing to compare

Left: Dwarf conifers are an ideal choice for the smaller garden. Right: Lawson's Cypress 'Triomphe de Boskoop' makes a dense hedge that is easy to care for.

with the Leyland Cypress, *Cupressocyparis×leylandii*. This vigorous hybrid has an amazing growth rate – up to 15 m (50 ft) in ten to fifteen years. It was first introduced to the home gardener some thirty years ago and is now the most widely planted hedging subject of all. It can be clipped well at any height from 2 m (6 ft) upwards.

Since its introduction, several distinctive forms have appeared, including 'Stapehill', with denser growth than the type, and 'Green Spire', with brighter green foliage.

Other hedging conifers, slower in growth but possibly more suited to the smaller garden, are some of the forms of Lawson's Cypress mentioned on page 37. Many of these make dense, impenetrable screens or windbreaks. *Thuya plicata*, formerly high in the charts as a hedging tree, has been largely superseded in popularity by the dynamic 'leylandii'.

Yew is the most easily managed and labour-saving tree of all when used for hedging. Clipping presents few problems until the hedge reaches maturity (usually in about ten to fifteen years from planting). Even then the operation will entail only the removal of 2.5–5 cm (1–2 in) of annual growth.

A yew hedge grows fairly fast in its early stages – up to 15 cm (6 in) in height and girth annually – it slows down considerably after this. It therefore is a long-term investment and many of us would not be prepared to wait for it to reach maturity, as this takes 10 years or more. Yew hedges should be trimmed only lightly to retain their dense growth.

There are quite a few other plants that need little care and clipping because of their comparatively slow rate of growth and compact, dense habit. Box is one of these. Once established, it needs very little atten-

tion. The common box, *Buxus semper-virens*, is the best for hedging. 'Gold Tip', with leaves splashed with yellow, and 'Handsworthensis', with upright growth, are the two kinds most commonly used. 'Suffruticosa' is the dwarf edging box, once widely cultivated as a formal edging and used in Tudor 'knot' gardens. Today, however, looking after garden features of this kind is too time-consuming an operation for most part-time gardeners, and it is wiser to keep your hedging plans as simple as possible.

Many evergreen flowering shrubs make colourful and decorative hedges that will need clipping only once a year – normally as soon as the flowers fade. The barberries, for example, include many forms that are ideal for this purpose. The vigorous *Berberis stenophylla* makes a strikingly beautiful hedge, with its long arching sprays of orange-yellow blossom in spring. The flowering shoots should be trimmed back hard after the flowers are over. This will also help to keep the hedge well-furnished at its base.

Two other good species are *B. darwinii* and *B. julianae*. These are more compact and have larger leaves than *stenophylla*. The flowers are orange and lemon-yellow respectively.

A yew hedge needs little clipping and looks very impressive, though it takes years to reach this stage.

The Mexican Orange, *Choisya ternata*, makes a dense and intensely fragrant hedge and will flourish in a shady situation. The shiny, three-lobed dark green leaves make a perfect foil for the cream waxy-textured flowers, which have a penetrating orange-blossom perfume. These appear from late spring to early summer, with a repeat performance later in the year. The Mexican Orange does well in the milder coastal districts of Britain, but is not suitable for cold, exposed situations.

The cotoneaster species, too, include many that make good evergreen hedges. The small white flowers are pretty but the main attraction of these shrubs lies in the abundant crops of scarlet berries that persist well into winter. *Cotoneaster franchetii, C. henryana* and *C. simonsii* are three of the best for hedging. All have handsome dark green foliage and bear their scarlet boot-button berries in great profusion.

The firethorns *Pyracantha* also include a number of useful evergreen berrying shrubs for hedging. Their spiny stems and dense growth make a hedge that is almost impenetrable by man or beast. Most of the *Pyracantha* species, including *P. gibbsii* and *P. rogersiana*, are good for hedging, but the best of all is 'Orange Glow', a vigorous cultivar with an abundance of orange-red berries.

None of the hedges mentioned should need clipping more than once a year. You should carry out this task with flowering types when they have finished their display, and with non-flowering kinds at the end of summer, in August or early September.

Where a dividing hedge is needed between different sections of the garden as, for example, between a pleasure garden and the fruit or vegetable plot, cordon or espalier fruit trees can be used to advantage. As well as their fruit, you can also enjoy the decorative blossom in spring which can rival the beauty of many ornamental flowering trees and shrubs. Cordons are grown on single, double or triple main stems and can be planted as little as 75 cm (2½ ft) apart, either at an angle of 45° (single cordons) or vertically (double and triple cordons). Espaliers have their side branches trained horizontally at intervals of about 60cm (2 ft)

Top: These shears are worked with one hand, and are ideal for small shrubs, such as lavender or rosemary; they are also a boon to the disabled gardener. Above: These shears have a notched blade for cutting thick stems. Below: A mains-operated hedge trimmer.

from a central upright stem and are planted 4.5–6 m (15–20 ft) apart. Apples and pears grow and crop well in cordon or espalier form.

Both forms are trained on wires, stretched between posts at intervals of not more than 3 m (10 ft). Pruning is not an arduous task, consisting of shortening side growths on the main stems to six or seven leaves in July with a further cutting back to two or three buds in late autumn or early winter. These operations encourage the formation of fruiting spurs.

A screen of this nature can serve a triple function, not only providing delicious fresh fruit but also being decorative and labour-saving. Such features are important when choosing trees or shrubs for any part of the garden. Although some may have a spectacular display, it is often short-lived. Those of the greatest value in the garden are the ones that either flower over a long period or provide a bonus, later in the year, in the shape of edible fruit or attractive berries, bark or autumn colour.

Hedging Tools

For gardens of moderate size, a good pair of garden shears should be sufficient for the job of hedge-trimming. Buy the best you can afford and make sure you get a pair with a notched blade for cutting through tough stems and small branches, essential where larger hedges such as beech, laurel or holly are being dealt with.

Lighter types of shears with shorter blades, some of which work with a one-handed, scissor-type action, can be useful for keeping small hedges in trim, such as those of lavender, box, or rosemary.

For gardens of above average size it will pay to invest in a powered hedge trimmer of some kind. This can be a great labour-saver where long stretches of hedge need clipping and also makes the cultivation of more demanding hedging shrubs, such as privet and lonicera, a much more practical proposition.

Several kinds of electric hedge trimmers are obtainable, with a choice of both mains and battery power. The latter are normally lighter in weight, easier to use, and ideal for small hedges; also they are safer, as there is no cable to get in the way.

5 · Climbing Plants and Wall Shrubs

Climbing plants are particularly valuable, since they provide colourful cover for walls, fences, pergolas and garden sheds, and, particularly where space is limited, offer what amounts almost to an extra dimension. Climbers are divided into several categories: mostly self-supporting clingers and twiners, wall shrubs and other kinds, which will need the support of wires or a trellis, and also require tying in as they grow.

It is the plants in the first two classes that will be of the greatest interest where the saving of labour is concerned, and it is these that are mainly featured in the list that follows. Also worth growing, however, are some of the wall shrubs, such as the Japanese quince, *Chaenomeles speciosa*, and the firethorns, or pyracanthas, which need supporting and tying only until the basic branch framework has developed. After this, they will stand without support, and will need only the same kind of pruning as any other free-standing shrub. See Pruning, page 19.

There are various kinds of support for climbing plants. Some, such as the ivies and Virginia creepers, will be satisfied with a wall or fence, since the former support themselves by aerial roots, the latter by sucker pads. For the types that need tying in to a support, alternatives are wooden trellis, wire or plastic netting, or wires strained to vine eyes at horizontal or vertical intervals. For smaller shrubs, such as climbing roses or

Pyracantha 'Orange Glow' and 'Lalandei', whose pretty flowers are followed by these showy berries.

the less rampant clematis, the special wall nails, with a lead strip that secures the stems of the plants to the wall, will be sufficient.

Some climbers are happiest if they are allowed to scramble through the branches of a host plant. For example, vigorous clematis species, such as *C. montana*, can be given the support of a wall shrub such as one of the firethorns, mentioned above. This ability can also be exploited in other parts of the garden where a trouble-free display is desired. Some of the more rampant clematis species will make a delightful garden picture climbing through the branches of an old apple or pear tree, while the climbing rose 'Kiftsgate', given a tall tree as a support, will quickly reach a height of 12m (40ft) or more and scent the air with its rich perfume when the masses of single cream flowers appear in late summer.

When climbers are being planted against a wall, it should always be remembered that the conditions surrounding its base are far from ideal. The soil will receive less than the normal amount of moisture, particularly when sited against a house wall if the roof above has an overhang, and where new houses are concerned, there will almost certainly be a lot of brick and cement rubble which has accumulated there during building operations.

It is better, therefore, to plant the climber 30–45 cm (1–1½ ft) away from the wall, paying careful attention to the preparation of the planting hole. Ideally, this should not be less than 60 cm (2 ft) square and 60 cm (2 ft) deep. It will pay, too, to replace the original soil from the hole with compost or good soil from another part of the garden, fortified with a few handfuls of bonemeal.

Easy-care climbers

The initials 'SS' indicate that the climber is self-supporting; other climbers require tying in to trellis, wires or wall nails, at least in their early stages.

Actinidia   Twiner
This is a group of vigorous climbing shrubs that will quickly cover large areas of wall or fence and act as camouflage for tall tree stumps or other unsightly objects. *Actinidia chinensis*, the Chinese Gooseberry, whose fruits are edible, will reach heights of 9m (30ft) or more. It has handsome heart-shaped leaves up to 20 cm (8 in) in length. The small, creamy-white flowers are followed

by fragrant oval fruits, which resemble brownish gooseberries. The other species most often seen is *A. kolomikta*, noteworthy for the unusual harlequin colouring of its leaves, which are horizontally banded with green, white and pink.
Soil – any
Sun or part shade

Aristolochia macrophylla   Twiner
This vigorous twining shrub is popularly known as the 'Dutchman's Pipe', on account of its unusual purple and yellow tubular flowers, which look like miniature saxophones.
Soil – any
Sun or part shade

Campsis radicans   Clinger
The exotic-looking climber, popularly known as the Trumpet Vine, bears clusters of vivid orange and scarlet trumpet-shaped flowers, 5–8 cm (2

–3 in) long, in late summer and early autumn. It clings by means of aerial roots on its stems, but may need supplementary support at first. It does best on a warm south or west wall.
Soil – rich, well-drained
Sun

Clematis   Twiner
This lovely group of plants has been justly called 'the queen of climbers'. Clematis soon support themselves by their twining leaf stalks and, as already mentioned, the more vigorous kinds can be used in conjunction with a host plant – either a shrub or an old tree. In general, it is the species that are the most vigorous, although there are also many fine, strong-growing hybrids. Clematis like their roots in moist shade and their heads in the sun, although many will also flower and flourish on a north-facing wall.

Species:
C. flammula An extremely vigorous species growing up to 5 m (16 ft) tall, with clusters of small but very fragrant white flowers from late summer through autumn. This species prefers a warm, sheltered south- or west-facing wall.
C. macropetala This is a useful species for growing on a pergola as its ultimate height is around 2.5 m (8 ft). The double flowers are violet-blue; they appear in early summer and are followed by decorative silky seedheads.
C. montana The best-known and most popular of the clematis species, so vigorous that its shoots will reach roof level in two seasons and cover a great deal of wall space. It does well on a northerly aspect. The two best forms are 'Rubens', with bronzy foliage and pale pink flowers, and 'Elizabeth', similar in appearance and habit, but with slightly larger flowers. The flowers appear in May and have a distinctive vanilla-like fragrance.
C. orientalis Often known as the Orange-peel Clematis, on account of its thick yellow sepals. This vigorous

Left: Chaenomeles speciosa. *Right*: Clematis *'Lasurstern' supports itself by scrambling through the branches of the Snowball Bush* Viburnum opulus.

species reaches heights of up to 6 m (20 ft). The yellow bell-shaped flowers are followed by silky seedheads.

C. tangutica This species is particularly noteworthy for the beauty of its yellow flowers, like miniature Chinese lanterns, as well as for the masses of silvery silken seedheads which follow them. It makes a first-rate subject for low walls and fences.

LARGE FLOWERED HYBRIDS:
The number of different kinds of large-flowered hybrid clematis must run into three figures, so only a selection can be given here. 'Jackmanii' is the best-known of these, with large violet flowers 10–12 cm (4–5 in) across. Others that deserve a place in any garden are 'Hagley Hybrid', a free flowering clematis, whose shell-pink flowers, produced in great abundance, have contrasting brown anthers; 'Lasurstern', possibly the loveliest lavender blue form, with striking white stamens; 'Marie Boisselot' (also called 'Mme Lecoultre'), the finest white; 'Mrs Cholmondeley', whose large pale blue flowers are freely produced; and 'Nelly Moser', second only to 'Jackmanii' in popularity, whose large pale mauve-pink flowers have their petals banded with carmine. The finest double is 'Vyvan Pennell' with flowers of a deep violet blue.
Soil – moist, well drained
Sun or part shade

Hedera (Ivy)   Clinger (SS)
All the ivies described in Ground Cover Plants, page 34, make first-rate evergreen climbers. They will thrive in the poorest of soils and in any aspect or situation. For creating an illusion of sunlight on a cheerless north wall, nothing can surpass a golden variegated ivy, such as *Hedera colchica* 'Variegata', the gold-splashed variety of the Persian ivy.
Soil – any
Sun or shade

Hydrangea petiolaris   Clinger (SS)
Popularly known as the Japanese Climbing Hydrangea, this interesting

Left: Summer Jasmine, Jasminum officinale, *climbs by twining. Its small white flowers are exceptionally fragrant.*
Right: Hydrangea petiolaris *supports itself by means of aerial roots.*

self-clinging wall shrub deserves to be better known, since it will quickly cover a north wall and produce masses of white or greenish white hydrangea flowers in June.
Soil – any
Sun or part shade

Jasminum (Jasmine)   Twiner
Several species of jasmine make attractive wall shrubs. The winter-flowering species, *Jasminum nudiflorum*, bears its yellow blossom from November to February. It can be grown on a north-facing or shaded wall. The Summer Jasmine, *J. officinale*, is a vigorous twiner which produces masses of small white intensely fragrant flowers from June to September. Its rather untidy and straggling habit of growth makes this climber more suitable for growing through trees or over sheds or other outbuildings.
Soil – fairly rich
Sun

Lonicera (Honeysuckle)   Twiner (SS)
These popular climbers are grown as much for the perfume of their tubular flowers as for their decorative display. Cultivars of our native Woodbine, *Lonicera periclymenum*, are among the most fragrant, although some other species and hybrids are showier and more colourful. Of the former, 'Belgica' and 'Serotina', respectively the early and late Dutch honeysuckles, are the most widely grown. Both have flowers of reddish purple and yellow which are borne in May and June by 'Belgica' and from July to October by 'Serotina'.
Soil – any
Part shade

Parthenocissus   Twiner (SS)
These climbers, formerly grouped under *Vitis*, support themselves by twining leaf tendrils, or in some cases by sucker pads. The species include *Parthenocissus quinquefolia*, the true Virginia Creeper, and the Boston

Ivy, *P. tricuspidata*, often confused with the former. Both are very vigorous, with spectacular orange and scarlet autumn leaf colour.
Soil – any
Sun or part shade

Vitis   Twiner (SS)
The ornamental vines, which support themselves by twining tendrils, are vigorous climbers which, in favourable seasons, produce bunches of small edible grapes. They are, however, grown primarily for the beauty of their foliage. The most eye-catching species is the Japanese Glory Vine, *Vitis coignetiae*, with rounded leaves up to 30 cm (1 ft) across. These turn a striking scarlet and crimson in autumn. Several forms of the wine grape, *V. vinifera*, also make attractive wall climbers, among them 'Incana', the Dusty Miller Grape, with black fruits and foliage dusted with a white down, and 'Purpurea', the Teinturier grape, with reddish leaves deepening to a rich purple by the end of summer.
Soil – any
Sun

Wisteria   Twiner (SS)
The wisterias are undoubtedly the most showy and colourful of all climbing shrubs. They support themselves by means of twining stems and their long tassels of pea flowers, lilac purple in most forms, are a magnificent sight when they festoon the branches in May and June. The pinnate foliage, too is always attractive, especially so as it first unfurls, when it is a lovely golden yellow in colour. *Wisteria sinensis* is the most popular species, with flower clusters 20–30 cm (8–12 in) long. These appear before the leaves. The white form, 'Alba', is also well worth growing. *W. floribunda*, the Japanese Wisteria, has the most striking cultivar of all, 'Macrobotrys', with pendant lilac flower trusses up to 1 m (3 ft) long. All wisteria flowers have a spicy scent, rather like that of lupins.
Soil – good loam
Sun

Left: Lilac-purple tassels of wisteria provide a welcome display in late spring.
*Right: Well-chosen climbers (*Vitis inconstans *and* Clematis 'Jackmanii'*) add an extra dimension to this garden.*

6 · Herbaceous Borders and Shrubs

In its original form, a herbaceous border was a garden feature planted exclusively with herbaceous perennials (plants that normally die down each winter but spring up again from the base the following year). The present trend, however, is to include only perennials that are relatively trouble-free and undemanding, requiring minimum tying, staking, dividing up and replanting. Their display can be supplemented with other similarly labour-saving plants, such as summer-flowering bulbs, together with shrubs of compact habit, ground cover plants and a selection of the old-fashioned shrub roses.

It will save a considerable amount of work in the long run if the site for the border is carefully prepared, since most of the plants that will be growing there will be of a permanent or semi-permanent nature. The ground should be dug over to a spade's depth, after which the subsoil is loosened with a fork and as many weeds as possible removed in the process. At this stage, well-rotted manure, compost or other humus-rich material should be dug in. A week or so before planting out the border, a dressing of bonemeal, at the rate of $120\,g/m^2$ (4 oz/sq yd) should be forked in.

Most perennials and shrubs can be planted at any time during autumn and winter as long as the soil is in a suitable condition – neither waterlogged nor frozen rock-hard. The exceptions, in the main, are grey- and

A herbaceous border stocked with well-chosen trouble-free plants will fill the garden with colour for many months.

silver-leafed shrubs, such as lavender, cotton lavender, phlomis and helichrysum, which are best planted in early spring. Conifers, too, seem to settle in more quickly when planted either in late autumn or late spring. Container-grown plants can be used for filling in gaps at any time of the year.

To obtain the best effect, the plants should be planted in groups rather than singly, with the exception of very large shrubs or those used as focal plantings. As a rough guide, groups of three of the same type of shrubs and the larger perennials, and up to six of the smaller varieties, will look attractive, helping to avoid a 'spotty' appearance.

A well-planned mixed border will be full of colour from late spring to mid-autumn. The display can be extended by including winter flowering shrubs like Witch-hazel, wintersweet and *Viburnum fragrans*, and perennials such as bergenias and the Christmas and Lenten roses, *Helleborus niger* and *H. orientalis*.

The smaller and more compact varieties of favourite border plants such as dwarf Michaelmas daisies and golden rod are virtually self-supporting. Other plants will need only a few twiggy sticks for support. These should be inserted round them when growth starts in spring. By the time the plants reach the flowering stage, the sticks will be completely hidden by the foliage.

For taller border plants that need support, for example Michaelmas daisies, dahlias, border chrysanthemums and the taller delphiniums, you can buy metal plant rings.

Labour-Saving Perennials

The two figures after each plant's name give its approximate height and spread when mature.

Late Spring and Early Summer

Alyssum saxatile
Rock Madwort
25×30 cm (10 in×1 ft)
This is a perennial relation of the popular annual white alyssum. It is normally grown in the rock garden but also makes a useful subject for the front of a border. It bears masses of golden-yellow flowers from April to June.
Soil – any
Sun

Aquilegia
Columbine
60×30 cm (2×1 ft)
The bonnet-shaped flowers of these attractive perennials are perfectly complemented by the masses of finely-cut ferny foliage. 'Crimson Star' is a fine cultivar, with long-spurred crimson and white flowers in May and June.
Soil – any
Sun

Bergenia
Giant Saxifrage
See Ground Cover Plants, page 32.

Brunnera macrophylla
Giant Forget-me-not
45×45 cm (1½×1½ ft)
The popular name aptly describes the sprays of large blue flowers borne by this handsome border plant. The flowers are borne on 45 cm (1½ ft) stems in April and May.
Soil – any
Sun or part shade

Convallaria majalis
Lily-of-the-Valley
25 cm (10 in) spreading
A deservedly popular perennial for the shadier parts of the border. It spreads rapidly, given suitable condi-tions of moisture and shade. Flowers appear in late May and early June.

Dicentra spectabilis
Bleeding Heart
60×45 cm (2×1½ ft)
Rose-red, locket-shaped flowers dangle from arching stems above finely cut foliage in late spring and early summer.
Soil – well-drained
Sun or part shade

Helleborus
Hellebore
Up to 60×60 cm (2×2 ft)
The various species of hellebore in-clude the Christmas Rose, *Helleborus niger* and the Lenten Rose, *H. orienta-lis*. These will provide colour in the border from December to the end of March. The most outstanding spe-cies, however, is *H. corsicus* with striking coarsely-toothed blueish foliage and huge clusters of apple-green flowers in February.
Soil – moist, rich loam
Sun or part shade

Iberis sempervirens
Perennial Candytuft
20×20 cm (8×8 in)
This is mostly seen in the rock garden but is equally attractive at the edge of a border. It produces its flat heads of pure white flowers from late spring to early summer.
Soil – any
Sun

Iris germanica
Flag Iris (and other bearded irises)
Up to 1 m (3 ft)
These irises make a beautiful display in late spring, compensating for their rather short flowering season by their beauty of form and brilliant colour-ing. They are extremely hardy and will thrive in most types of soil. Popular cultivars include 'Aline', sky-blue; 'Black Swan', black with a brown-tipped beard; 'Cliffs of Dover', white; 'Chinese Coral', pinkish-orange; 'Olympic Torch', golden bronze; 'Staten Island', mahogany and yellow; and 'White City', white. A suitable choice of varieties will pro-

Left: Lenten Rose, Helleborus orientalis. *Right:* Meconopsis betonicifolia.

vide flowers from late May to July.
Soil – well-drained
Sun

Meconopsis betonicifolia
Blue Poppy
1 m (3 ft)
The blue poppy-like flowers with

striking golden stamens are borne throughout June.
Soil – lime-free, moist
Part shade

Pulmonaria
Lungwort
30×30 cm (1×1 ft)

Useful semi-evergreen perennials for the front of the border. *Pulmonaria angustifolia* has narrow leaves and gentian-blue flowers; *P. saccharata* (Bethlehem Sage) has deep green leaves mottled with white. Its pink flowers turn blue as they mature. 'Mrs. Moon' and 'Pink Dawn' are

improvements on the type. Both species make good ground cover; they flower in April and May.

Soil – any
Part or full shade

Pulsatilla vulgaris
Pasque Flower
20×30 cm (8 in×1 ft)
Formerly known as *Anemone pulsatilla*, this charming little plant has pendent, purple, bell-shaped flowers covered with a silvery down, followed by attractive silken seedheads. It flowers in May and June.

Soil – any
Sun

Symphytum grandiflorum
See Ground Cover Plants, page 35.

Summer

Acanthus
Bear's Breeches
Up to 1.5 m×60 cm (5×2 ft)
Evergreen perennials with finely sculptured foliage and majestic spikes of purple and white hooded flowers. Of the two species, *Acanthus spinosus* is more striking than *A. mollis*. Both flower in July.

Soil – any
Sun or shade

Achillea
Yarrow
Some up to 1.2×1.2 m (4×4 ft)
The achilleas are a large group of border perennials with dainty ferny foliage. The flat flower heads provide contrast in the border. They also dry well for winter arrangements. Good named kinds include the popular 'Gold Plate', with golden yellow flower heads on 1.2 m (4 ft) stems; 'Coronation Gold', similar to but more compact than the former; 'Moonshine' with silvery foliage and pale yellow flowers; and 'Taygetea', with grey leaves and lemon-yellow flowers. Most flower between June and August.

Soil – any
Sun

Alchemilla mollis
See Ground Cover Plants, page 32.

Anthemis
Camomile
1 m×45 cm (3×1½ ft)
These attractive border plants pro-

duce their yellow daisy flowers over an exceptionally long period, from midsummer to September. 'Beauty of Grallagh', 'E. C. Buxton' and 'Grallagh Gold' are three of the best hybrid cultivars.

Soil – well-drained
Sun

Aruncus sylvester
Goat's Beard
1.2 m×60 cm (4×2 ft)
These tall plants, formerly classed with the spiraeas, bear large plumes of creamy-white blossom around midsummer, to which their finely-cut foliage provides an attractive foil.

Soil – moist
Sun or shade

Astilbe
False Goat's Beard
Up to 1 m (3 ft)
These bear conspicuous spikes of feathery flowers in a wide range of vivid colours. The best named garden forms are hybrids and include the pure white 'Bridal Veil'; 'Fanal', a fine crimson; 'Ostrich Plume', rich pink; and 'Red Sentinel', scarlet-red. Flowers in July and August.

Soil – moist
Sun or shade

Campanula
Bellflower
Up to 1.5 m (5 ft)×60 cm (2 ft)
There are many different kinds of campanula, ranging from rock plants only a few inches tall to the stately *Campanula lactiflora*, 1.5 m (5 ft) in height, which, in spite of its considerable stature, needs no support. This species has pale lavender-blue, bell-shaped flowers. *C. glomerata*, with rounded heads of violet flowers is a popular species that remains in flower for a very long time. Other popular kinds include 'Loddon Anna', a delightful pink cultivar of *C. lactiflora*, and *C. persicifolia*, a species that averages 1 m (3 ft) in height and includes one of the finest campanulas – 'Telham Beauty', with tall spires of large, rich blue flowers. Most campanulas flower in June and July.

Soil – deep, moist
Sun or part shade

Chrysanthemum maximum
Shasta Daisy
1 m×30 cm (3×1 ft), spreading

A tough, vigorous plant with a rapid rate of spread. There are kinds with single and double daisy flowers all of which cut well. 'Esther Read', double white; 'Everest', a fine white single; 'Wirral Supreme', another pure white double; and 'Beaute Nivelloise,' with attractively fringed petals, are all good garden forms. Normally self-supporting, these may need the help of a few twiggy sticks in exposed situations. Flowers are borne from June to August.

Soil – any
Sun

Coreopsis
Up to 75 cm (2½ ft)×30 cm (1 ft)
Useful perennials with golden daisy-like flowers that need a sunny situation. 'Badengold', 'Mayfield Giant' and 'Sunburst' are all fine cultivars; 'Goldfink' is a delightful dwarf variety with deep yellow flowers. They flower from July to September.

Soil – any
Sun

Delphinium
Belladonna Hybrids
1 m×45 cm (3×1½ ft)
The taller hybrid delphiniums, with their towering 2 m (6 ft) flower spikes, need too much attention to warrant their inclusion in this list, outstandingly beautiful though they undoubtedly are. For the labour-saving border, the Belladonna Hybrids, which rarely exceed 1 m (3 ft) in height, are a much better choice. Good named forms of these are 'Blue Bees', pale blue; 'Pink Sensation', clear pink; and 'Wendy', deep blue. Perhaps more beautiful still is the 'Blue Fountains' strain, which is easy to raise from seed and produces sturdy plants needing no staking, with flower spikes that rival those of the largest varieties. Belladonna Hybrids flower in June and July.

Soil – rich, well-drained
Sun

Echinacea purpurea (*Rudbeckia purpurea*)
Strikingly handsome border plants whose daisy-like flowers have a central conical eye. Outstanding culti-

Astilbe *'Bressingham Beauty'; like all the astilbes, it prefers a moist site.*

vars are 'The King' with crimson flowers and 'Goldquelle' a double form, with yellow flowers.
Soil – any
Sun or part shade

Erigeron
Fleabane
Up to 60×30 cm (2×1 ft)
The pink or mauve flowers resemble those of the Michaelmas daisies. They generally flower from June to August. 'Felicity', deep pink; 'Sincerity', pale mauve; and 'Darkest of All', deep violet-blue, are all worth growing.
Soil – any
Sun

Geum borisii *'Lady Stratheden'*.

Eryngium
Sea Holly
Up to 1.2 m×60 cm (4×2 ft)
The eryngiums are good plants for exposed situations. The hybrid *Eryngium×oliverianum* is particularly striking, with its metallic blue thistle-like flowers and stems. *E. tripartitum* is taller, with candelabra-like sprays of blue flowers. In both cases, the flowers appear from July to August.
Soil – light
Sun

Geranium
Crane's Bill
Up to 60×45 cm (2×1½ ft)
These hardy border plants should not be confused with the tender bedding 'geranium' whose correct title

is 'zonal pelargonium'. Some, such as *Geranium endressii*, are good ground-cover plants that flower almost continuously throughout the summer. 'Claridge Druce', with grey-green leaves and magenta-pink flowers, 'Wargrave Pink' and 'Johnson's Blue' are all vigorous and long-flowering. None of these exceed 60 cm (2 ft) in height.
Soil – any
Sun or part shade

Geum
Avens
60×30 cm (2×1 ft)
A very old favourite among border plants, which starts to flower in early June and continues in bloom until August. Those most commonly seen

are cultivars of *Geum borisii* and include 'Fire Opal', with brilliant orange flowers; 'Lady Stratheden', with yellow blooms; and 'Red Wings', whose bright red flowers are flushed with orange.
Soil – any
Sun

Gypsophila
Up to 1.2×1 m (4×3 ft)
The species most often seen in the border is *Gypsophila paniculata*, with clouds of tiny flowers in dainty sprays. The white-flowered 'Bristol Fairy' is the best-known form, but the dwarf 'Rosy Veil' with pink flowers is also popular. The plants flower from July to August.
Soil – chalky
Sun

Helenium
1 m×30 cm (3×1 ft)
A popular group of plants providing plenty of colour. 'Bruno', with deep mahogany red flowers from July to September; 'Crimson Beauty', flowering from June to August; and 'The Bishop', which bears rich yellow flowers with brown centres from July to September, are three of the more compact cultivars.
Soil – light, well-drained
Sun

Hemerocallis
Day Lily
Up to 1.2 m×90 cm (4×3 ft)
These easily grown members of the lily family produce large clumps of sword-like foliage, bearing masses of lily flowers on tall stems over a period of many weeks in summer. Each flower lasts for a day or two only, then another opens – hence the popular name. The group contains a wide range of colours from palest yellow through shades of orange to deep mahogany red. Of the numerous garden hybrids, the following would make a good representative selection: 'Burning Daylight', with deep orange flowers flushed with copper, appearing from July to August; 'Delicate Splendour', with pale yellow to white flowers from July to September; 'Katherine Ormerod' bearing bright red flowers from July to September; 'Glowing Gold', with bright orange flowers from July to September; and 'Pink Damask', with

coppery pink flowers from July to August.
Soil – any
Sun or part shade

Hosta
See Ground-Cover Plants, page 34.

Kniphofia
Red Hot Poker
Up to 1.2 m (4 ft)×60 cm (2 ft)
These are popular border plants, whose flower spikes, or 'pokers', can be white, yellow, or varying shades of orange, coral or scarlet. The clumps of grassy foliage remain decorative at all times. 'Sunset', with orange pokers; 'Royal Standard', with scarlet and yellow pokers and 'St. Cross', with deep yellow pokers are outstanding among the larger kinds. These flower from June to July. *Kniphofia galpinii*, with orange-yellow flowers, is a useful late-flowering species (September–October). 'Maid of Orleans' bears slender spikes of ivory white flowers from July to September.
Soil – any
Sun

Liatris
Gay Feather
60×30 cm (2×1 ft)
This medium-sized perennial, with its long spikes of purple flowers, makes a showy subject for the middle of the border. The flowers appear from July to September. It is unusual in being one of the few plants whose flower spikes open from the tip downwards. They make attractive and long-lasting cut flowers.
Soil – well-drained
Sun or part shade

Lysimachia
Loosestrife
1 m×45 cm (3×1½ ft)
The Yellow Loosestrife, *Lysimachia punctata*, is an old cottage-garden favourite. The yellowish cup-shaped flowers resemble those of its close relation Creeping Jenny, but they are borne in loose spikes on tall, upright stems, during June and July. *L. clethroides*, a lesser-known species, has attractive bottle-brush-like spikes of small, white, star-shaped flowers, in July and August.
Soil – any
Sun or part shade

Macleaya cordata
Plume Poppy
Up to 2.5×1 m (8×3 ft)
An unusual member of the large poppy family which, in spite of its great height, stands up well without support. The flowers are small and creamy-white, borne in small feathery clusters. The plume poppy is equally noteworthy for the beauty of its lobed blueish foliage, silvered on the reverse. An ideal plant for the back of the border but once established, it spreads very rapidly. The flowers appear in August.
Soil – any
Sun or part shade

Monarda didyma
Sweet Bergamot
90×38 cm (3 ft×15 in)
A colourful asset to any border. This aromatic herb is used to impart its distinctive flavour to a distinguished blend of tea. In the type plant the whorls of hooded flowers are a vivid scarlet. 'Blue Stocking', with violet-purple flowers, and 'Croftway Pink', with rose-pink blooms, are attractive variants. The flowers appear from June to August.
Soil – any
Sun or part shade

Nepeta×faassenii
Catmint
45×30 cm (1×1½ ft)
Also known as *N. mussinii*, this is a vigorous grey-leaved aromatic perennial, which flowers over a very long period and makes an excellent edging plant. The flower spikes are lavender-blue in colour and the more vigorous 'Six Hills Variety' grows up to about 1 m (3 ft) tall. The flowers are borne from May to September.
Soil – any
Sun

Penstemon
Up to 1 m×60 cm (3×2 ft)
There are various species of penstemon suitable for the border, all with attractive foxglove-type flowers in a wide range of colours. 'Evelyn', with pink flowers, and 'Garnet', with deep red blooms, are both good forms. 'Blue Gem' has flowers of a lovely sky blue. All flower from July to September.
Soil – any
Sun or part shade

Phlox paniculata
Border Phlox
Up to 1 m×60 cm (3×2 ft)
Also known as *P. decussata*, these popular border plants flower continuously from July well into September. There is a large choice of varieties in an equally wide range of colours. A representative selection would include 'Border Gem', deep violet; 'Brigadier', orange-red; 'Rembrandt', pure white; 'Tempest', carmine-pink; and 'Vintage Wine', reddish purple. In exposed situations, 'Mia Ruys', white, and 'Otley Purple' which are more compact than the first five mentioned, would be a better choice.
Soil – rich, well-drained
Sun or part shade

Polygonum
See Ground Cover Plants, page 34.

Potentilla
Cinquefoil
60×60 cm (2×2 ft)
These attractive free-flowering plants have strawberry-like leaves and flowers. 'Gibson's Scarlet', a semi-prostrate form with bright red flowers; 'Roulette', with vivid red flowers tipped with yellow; and 'William Rollison' with orange-yellow semi-double blooms, are all worth a place in the border. The flowers are borne from June to September.
Soil – well-drained
Sun or part shade

Rudbeckia
Cone Flower
Up to 1 m×45 cm (3×1½ ft)
For trouble-free maintenance, plant only the smaller kinds which flower mainly in summer. The finest of these are named cultivars of *Rudbeckia fulgida deamii* which itself is a handsome plant, having bright yellow daisy-like flowers with a central black boss. 'Goldquelle' and 'Goldsturm' are both equally attractive; the flowers of the latter are a paler lemon-yellow. The flowering period is July to September.
Soil – any
Sun or part shade

Salvia
Sage
Up to 1 m×60 cm (3×2 ft)
The salvias form a large plant group.

In addition to the culinary sage, *Salvia officinalis*, whose variegated forms make fine edging plants, there are many other species and cultivars suitable for any position in the border. One of the most striking of these is *S. superba* (also known as *S. virgata nemerosa*), noteworthy for its dense spikes of purple flowers which retain their beauty even when they have faded, to a rich cinnamon-brown. *S. haematodes*, with pale blue flowers, is another species worth a place, while *S. argentea* is cultivated primarily for its silver-felted foliage. The flowers appear from July to August.
Soil – any
Sun

Sidalcea
Greek Mallow
1 m×60 cm (3×2 ft)
The mallow-like flowers of this perennial appear in a long succession

Sidalcea flowers over a long period.

from midsummer well into autumn. Sidalceas do not like disturbance. Good named cultivars include 'Rose Queen', with rose-pink flowers; 'Sussex Beauty', with clear pink blooms; and 'William Smith', with salmon pink flowers. The flowering period is from July to September.
Soil – any
Sun or part shade

Solidago
Golden Rod
Up to 1 m×45 cm (3×1½ ft)
Solidagos have plumes of tiny yellow flowers and are easy to grow. Although many of the older forms are rather uninteresting, as well as being tall and terribly invasive, the smaller and more compact introductions make excellent trouble-free plants. Among these are several dwarfs, 30 cm (1 ft) or less in height, such as 'Cloth of Gold' and 'Laurin'. On the taller side are 'Goldenmosa' with yellow, mimosa-like flowers

and 'Ledsham', a brilliant yellow golden rod of medium height. The plants flower from August to September.
Soil – any
Sun or part shade

Stachys
45×30 cm (1½×1 ft)
The best-known member of this species is *Stachys lanata*, whose flannel-textured leaves with their white woolly down have earned the plant its popular name of 'Lamb's Tongue'. This is an 'evergrey', useful for ground cover at the edge of the border. Since the small purple flowers are uninteresting, the newer cultivar 'Silver Carpet', a non-flowering form, is a great improvement on the type. *S. macrantha* 'Superba' (Betony) has much more striking blooms of a rich rosy mauve, which appear from July to August. The wrinkled hairy foliage is also attractive. This plant is sometimes known as *Betonica macrantha* or *B. grandiflora*.
Soil – any
Sun

Tradescantia x andersoniana
Spiderwort
45×45 cm (1½×1½ ft)
Most of the garden forms of this plant are hybrids, noteworthy for the exceptional length of their flowering season, which lasts from June to September. There are several good cultivars, including 'Bluestone', with bluish purple flowers; 'J.C. Weguelin', azure blue; 'Iris Prichard', rosy mauve; and an unusual semi-double mauve, 'Flore Pleno'.
Soil – any
Sun or part shade

Veronica
Speedwell
45×23 cm (1½ ft×9 in)
There are many species of veronica, ranging in height from a few centimetres to 1.5 m (5 ft) or more. The best for the trouble-free border are those of medium height such as *Veronica incana*, with silvery leaves and intense blue flower spikes; 'Crater Lake Blue', with ultramarine flowers; and 'Pavane', with grey foliage and pink flower spikes. These all flower from June to August.
Soil – light to medium loam
Sun or part shade

Autumn

Although the choice narrows considerably when border perennials for the autumn display are under consideration, there are still quite a number that will provide colour in abundance from September well into November. The most widely grown of these are the Michaelmas Daisies.

Anemone x hybrida
Japanese Anemone
Up to 1 m×45 cm (3×1½ ft)
Often listed as *A. japonica*, these are exceptionally fine plants with single or semi-double, satin-textured, chalice-shaped flowers. 'Louise Uhink' is a splendid semi-double white; 'Queen Charlotte' and 'Prince Henry' are two 'royals' with pale and deep pink flowers respectively. 'September Charm' is a pale pink single whose petals are tinged with mauve.
Soil – light to medium loam
Sun or shade

Aster
Michaelmas Daisy
Up to 1 m×45 cm (3×1½ ft)
This important group of border plants is an ideal choice for bringing down the curtain on the border display in a blaze of colour. The taller kinds should be avoided, as they need staking and tying. The dwarf kinds, not more than 15 cm (6 in) in height, are ideal for the edge of the border, and require no support, while those of medium height may need the support of a few twiggy sticks in exposed gardens. The cultivars in the *novi-belgii* group are mostly in the medium range, and a good choice would be 'Ada Ballard', with double mauve flowers; 'Crimson Brocade', deep red double; 'Jean', violet mauve; 'Carnival', crimson pink semi-double; and 'Raspberry Ripple', a carmine pink semi-double.

The dwarf hybrids, which are not more than 60 cm (2 ft) in height (most are shorter), are literally covered in bloom during their flowering period. Good cultivars include 'Blue Bouquet', with bright blue flowers; 'Jenny', reddish pink; and 'Snowsprite', a fine semi-double white. All the above-named flower between September and October.
Soil – any
Sun

Ceratostigma plumbaginoides
Leadwort
30×38 cm (1 ft×15 in)
This is a dwarf perennial plumbago that is completely hardy; it is sometimes classified as a sub-shrub. The flowers, borne in small clusters, appear from September to October and are a deep blue in colour. An added attraction is the rich rust-red colour of the leaves when they fade.
Soil – light
Sun

Chrysanthemum rubellum
75×45 cm (2½×1½ ft)
Although most of the hardy border chrysanthemums are summer flowering, this is one attractive species that blooms in autumn and is completely hardy. Good cultivars are 'Clara Curtis', with pink flowers; 'Mary Stoker', soft yellow; and 'Duchess of Edinburgh', rich chestnut-red. All bloom in October.
Soil – any
Sun

Clematis heracleifolia
1 m×45 cm (3×1½ ft)
This perennial is useful for the autumn border. The foliage is like that of a climbing species such as *montana*, and the blue flowers, which resemble the bells of hyacinths, are attractive and colourful. The hybrid 'Cote d'Azur' has flowers of a deeper blue than those of the type. The flowers appear during October.
Soil – alkaline
Sun or part shade

Helianthus decapetalus
Perennial Sunflower
1.2×60 cm (4×2 ft)
Perennial sunflowers have a reputation for invasiveness but newer forms are more compact and easily kept within bounds. They include 'Loddon Gold' and 'Capenoch Star', with double and single yellow flowers respectively. The flowers are borne in October.
Soil – any
Sun

Physostegia virginiana
Obedient Plant
75×60 cm (2½×2 ft)
This curious plant gets its popular name from the behaviour of its tubular flowers, each of which is on a kind

of ball-and-socket joint and stays put when moved in any direction. 'Vivid', with rose pink flowers, is the showiest cultivar. 'Alba', with white flowers, is also worth growing. Both flower in October.

Soil – any

Sun or part shade

Sedum
Stonecrop or Ice Plant
Up to 60×45 cm (2×1½ ft)
The sedums, with their fleshy leaves and large flat flower heads, are among the brightest jewels of the autumn border.The flowers of these plants attract butterflies in a similar way to those of the buddleias. 'Autumn Joy', with salmon pink flowers; 'Ruby Glow', deep ruby red; and 'Brilliant', bright pink, are three of the most outstanding forms. They flower from September to October.

Soil – well-drained

Sun or part shade

Labour-Saving Roses

Many gardeners are deterred from growing roses because their pruning seems to be a bewildering task surrounded by a great deal of mystique. Although not nearly as daunting a job as it might at first appear, the pruning of roses such as the floribundas and hybrid teas does require a fair amount of time and care, both in finding out the correct pruning method for the types and varieties of rose being grown, and in the actual pruning itself.

This is all very well if you insist on growing types such as the hybrid teas and if your aim is to produce perfect individual blooms. However, if you want to cut down on routine work choose the old shrub roses or their modern equivalents. With these, as in most other hardy shrubs, pruning consists merely of cutting out dead or diseased wood, or any shoots that are crossing or growing into the centre of the bush. Prune in March or early April; do not prune during a hard frost.

These labour-saving tactics will give you a riot of bloom with plentiful supplies for cutting, rather than a dozen flowers of more perfect shape.

The colour, form and fragrance of the old shrub roses is magnificent. Many of them bear decorative fruits, known as hips (or heps), in various shades of red, orange or yellow. In some kinds the hips are as large as small tomatoes, while in others they are flagon-shaped, or tapering, or covered in hairs.

Some shrub roses, such as *R. rubrifolia*, are grown primarily for the beauty of their foliage. The leaves of this rose are grey-green with a reddish-purple tinge. It is almost thornless and the single pink flowers are followed by clusters of reddish brown hips.

R. pterocantha is probably unique among garden shrubs in being cultivated for the appearance of its large, translucent scarlet thorns, which are extremely showy on the younger shoots. Other shrub roses, like the attractive Penzance Briars, have delightfully aromatic foliage and can be used to make a scented hedge, since they clip well and still produce a good crop of blooms.

Shrub roses will thrive in any fertile soil and are mostly very hardy, surviving cold winds and sharp frosts that often damage other roses. Some varieties grow up to 2 m (6 ft) high and reach the same width, while others are more compact, such as 'Cécile Brunner', which grows to a mere 60 cm (2 ft).

Planting
Bare-root roses may be planted at any time from late October to the end of March, but November planting gives the best results. Container-grown roses can be planted at any time of the year. Plant when the soil is easily worked, neither waterlogged nor too dry, and not during a frost. If conditions are not suitable when the roses arrive, 'heel them in' by burying their roots in a shallow trench until the situation improves. If there is a severe frost, do not remove the roses from their packing.

Break up the base of the planting holes to encourage good drainage and make sure that they are wide and deep enough to allow the roots to spread out comfortably. Plant so that the soil mark on the stem is just covered. You can mix a handful of bonemeal thoroughly with the soil before you return it to the hole. Firm in the rose by treading the soil. Plant shrub roses at least 1.5 m (5 ft) apart, unless they are to form a hedge, in which case they should go in about 75 cm (2½ ft) apart.

Cultivation
Shrub roses need little attention; a mulch of well-rotted compost, leaf-mould or moist peat can be applied to the soil in summer (make sure the soil is moist before you apply it) and if growth has not been good feed with a rose fertilizer in April, forking it beneath the mulch.

Old Shrub Roses

Alba Group
These are among the oldest roses known in garden cultivation, some dating back to Roman times. They are tough and vigorous and thrive in almost any kind of soil, including light sandy types. They are compact, bushy shrubs and their blooms are exceptionally fragrant, flat and packed with petals. The foliage is greyish-blue. 'Celestial', with clear pink flowers; 'Félicité Parmentier', double white; 'Great Maiden's Blush', soft pink; and 'Queen of Denmark', a deep rich pink, are among the best in this section. The albas bloom around midsummer and the flowers are followed by showy, scarlet, oval hips.

Bourbon Group
The Bourbon group contains some of the best of the old-fashioned roses, including the lovely shell rose, 'Mme Pierre Oger', with globular blooms of a delicate creamy pink; 'La Reine Victoria', deep pink; 'Mme Isaac Périère', double crimson; and 'Souvenir de la Malmaison', pale pink.

'Constance Spry', a beautiful clear pink fully double rose, is a noteworthy recent introduction to this category, while another popular Bourbon rose is the thornless 'Zéphirine Drouhin', whose vigorous growth makes it a useful wall shrub. It has masses of blooms of a dazzling pink.

Most of the Bourbons bloom more or less continuously throughout the summer and autumn. Their shapely flowers have a strong fragrance.

Centifolia Group
This group includes the old sweetly

Mixed borders of annuals and herbaceous perennials make a neat, attractive and trouble-free garden feature.

scented Cabbage Roses, so popular in Victorian gardens, and contains some of the oldest roses known in cultivation. 'Pink Cabbage' and 'White Provence' are the two that most approximate to the 'cabbage' description. The pale pink blooms of 'Fantin Latour' are flattened, with a button centre, while those of 'Tour de Malakoff' are deep lavender on opening, turning to shades of paler mauve, violet and grey as the flowers mature. The centifolias flower once, around midsummer.

China Rose Group
This group contains varieties and hybrids of *Rosa chinensis*, all of which flower freely from early summer to the end of the year. The gem of this collection is 'Cécile Brunner', a semi-dwarf bush with flowers like those of a miniature pink hybrid tea. Others in the group worth growing are 'Bloomfield Abundance', with miniature shell-pink flowers similar to those of 'Cécile Brunner'; 'Fellemberg', with its crimson-pink flowers in large clusters; and 'Jenny Wren', a newer hybrid, with clusters of coral-pink blooms. Also included is the unusual 'green' rose, *viridiflora*, whose flowers, blue-green in bud and streaked with brown at maturity, are great favourites with flower arrangers.

Damascena Group
Rosa damascena, the Damask Rose, flowers around midsummer, and is distinguished by the exceptionally rich fragrance of its blooms. It is these, in fact, that are used in the manufacture of attar of roses. 'Omar Khayyam', with flat pink blooms, was originally raised from the seed of a plant growing on the poet's grave. Other worthwhile forms include 'Blush Damask', lilac pink; 'Ispahan', rose pink; and 'Mme Hardy', white. All have fully double flowers.

Gallica Group
The gallicas, in general, are low-growing, with small pale green leaves and double or semi-double flowers that appear around midsummer. One of the best known is 'Versicolor', (also known as 'Rosa Mundi'), with gaily striped crimson and white blooms. Other colourful gallicas include 'Tuscany', whose crimson semi-

double blooms have showy golden stamens, and 'Belle de Crécy', with lovely lilac-pink double flowers, which mature to violet purple.

Moyesii Group
In the main, the *moyesii* roses are taller than most other shrub roses, with an elegant arching habit of growth. The flowers are single and vividly coloured, followed by decorative flask-shaped orange hips.

Rugosa group
The rugosas and their hybrids are among the most widely grown of the old shrub roses. They have a tough, disease-resistant constitution – they are almost immune to black spot – great vigour, attractive grey-green wrinkled foliage, fragrant flowers, decorative hips and colourful golden yellow autumn foliage. Pruned back hard, they produce an abundance of blooms from midsummer to autumn.

'Blanc Double de Coubert', with 'whiter than white' flowers that look as though they have been scissored

out of crêpe paper, is one of the loveliest.

Other shrub roses
More recent introductions possessing the vigour and ease of cultivation of their older relations include 'Fritz Nobis', which has masses of clove-scented semi-double salmon-pink blooms followed by decorative hips, and 'Nevada', one of the tallest and most productive of all the shrub roses, whose arching stems are massed with creamy-white single blooms, 10 cm (4 in) across.

Equally attractive are the hybrids of the Burnet Rose, known as the 'Frühlings' group. The star of this collection is 'Frühlingsgold', an early-flowering shrub rose whose creamy-yellow flowers have prominent golden stamens and are very sweetly scented.

Below: The beautiful shrub rose 'Nevada'. Right: The hardy hybrid rhododendrons thrive in moist peaty soils and need minimum care. This is 'Mrs. Furnival'.

SHRUBS FOR THE LABOUR-SAVING GARDEN

Labour-Saving Shrubs

The list below represents a selection of deciduous and evergreen shrubs whose flowers, foliage or decorative fruit should provide interest the whole year through. They have all received the Royal Horticultural Society Award of Garden Merit which means they have undergone tests in a wide variety of garden conditions, and will flourish in a wide range of climates.

Pruning Shrubs

The basic rule for pruning shrubs that flower on the previous year's wood is to prune them as soon as the blossom has faded. Examples are philadelphus, lilac and *Cytisus albus*. The old flowering shoots should be cut back hard to stimulate the growth of strong new wood, which will bear the flowers the following season. Take care to retain any new shoots that are present. Generally speaking, shrubs in this group bloom before summer.

Shrubs that flower on the current year's growth are normally pruned in late winter. These include many grey-leaved shrubs, such as olearia, santolina, senecio and caryopteris. Generally speaking, shrubs in this group flower after midsummer.

Slow-growing shrubs, such as camellias and rhododendrons, are ideal labour-savers, since they require little or no pruning. If you can spare the time, however, rhododendrons will benefit from the removal of the faded flower heads. This gives the new season's shoots a chance to get away quickly.

Shrubs for the Labour-Saving Garden

Under Pruning, X indicates that little or no pruning is needed, apart from occasional removal of dead, frost-damaged or straggly growths; F indicates that pruning should be done after the flowers have faded; and LW that it should be carried out in late winter.

The dimensions given are those the shrubs should reach after ten years in average garden conditions.

Key:
Deciduous
Evergreen
Semi-evergreen

Name	Height & Spread	Flowering Period	Description	Pruning
Acer palmatum 'Atropurpureum' JAPANESE MAPLE	200×150 cm (6×5 ft)	Foliage	Finely cut purple leaves. Good autumn colour.	X
Berberis thunbergii BARBERRY	150×130 cm (5×4½ ft)	May	Small pale yellow, red-tinged flowers in clusters. Scarlet autumn foliage and winter berries	F
Berberis darwinii	150×130 cm (5×4½ ft)	Apr/May	Small orange flowers, coral-pink in bud, profusely borne. Miniature holly-like foliage and purple berries.	F
Camellia x williamsii 'J.C. WILLIAMS'	250×120 cm (8×4 ft)	Feb/May	Large pale pink flowers with central cluster of golden stamens. Handsome polished foliage attractive all year through.	X
Caryopteris clandonensis BLUE SPIRAEA	120×100 cm (4×3 ft)	Aug/Oct	Compact grey-leaved shrub with violet-blue flowers in early autumn.	LW
Cercis siliquastrum JUDAS TREE	300×250 cm (10×8 ft)	May	Large shrub of tree-like habit whose bare branches are studded with clusters of purple pea-flowers in late spring. Attractive blue-green heart-shaped leaves.	X
Cistus ocymoides ROCK ROSE	50×100 cm (1½×3 ft)	June/Aug	Grey-green foliage makes a lovely setting for yellow flowers like small single roses.	X
Cytisus albus WHITE PORTUGAL BROOM	200×150 cm (6×5 ft)	May/June	White flowers massed in dainty sprays against grey-green foliage.	F
Daphne mezereum MEZERON	120×100 cm (4×3 ft)	Feb/Mar	One of the best winter-flowering shrubs with very fragrant purple flowers followed by scarlet berries.	X
Enkianthus campanulatus	200×120 cm (6×4 ft)	May	Creamy-yellow hanging bell-shaped flowers suffused with red. Striking autumn leaf colour.	X
Erica carnea 'Springwood White' WINTER HEATHER	20×30 cm (8 in ×1 ft)	Jan/Mar	White flowers with brown anthers. Dense spreading habit makes it a good ground cover plant.	F
Euonymus alata	150×120 cm (5×4 ft)	Foliage	Brilliant carmine autumn leaf colour and attractive corky winged bark in winter.	X

Fatsia japonica	150×150 cm (5×5 ft)	Oct/Nov	Handsome polished palmate leaves more than 30 cm (1 ft) across. Creamy drumstick flowers in clusters.	X
Fuchsia 'Mrs. Popple'	150×100 cm (5×3 ft)	June/Oct	One of the best hardy fuchsias. The large flowers have carmine sepals and a violet corolla.	LW
Garrya elliptica	200×150 cm (6×5 ft)	Jan/Feb	Decorative, long, jade-green catkins in winter.	X
Genista lydia	50×100 cm (1½×3 ft)	May/June	Useful rock garden shrub forming low hummock of grey-green stems massed with golden flowers in early summer.	X
Hebe pinguifolia 'Pagei'	50×100 cm (1½×3 ft)	May/June	Dwarf evergreen shrub with blue-green foliage and spikes of pearly-white flowers.	X
Hydrangea paniculata 'Grandiflora'	200×150 cm (6×5 ft)	Aug/Sept	Large pyramids of long-lasting creamy-white blooms turning pink as they fade.	LW
Hypericum patulum 'Hidcote' ROSE OF SHARON	120×100 cm (4×3 ft)	June/Oct	Large golden flowers like single roses with decorative stamens.	LW
Lavandula spica 'Hidcote' LAVENDER	50×50 cm (1½×1½ ft)	July/Sept	Compact form with striking deep blue flowers.	F
Magnolia soulangiana	450×450 cm (15×15 ft)	May	Best-known and most widely-grown magnolia. Purple-tinged white flowers on bare stems and branches.	X
Olearia haastii DAISY BUSH	100×100 cm (3×3 ft)	July/Sept	Attractive grey-leaved shrub that thrives in seaside and industrial areas.	LW
Osmanthus delavayii	150×200 cm (5×6 ft)	April	Small dark green leaves and masses of tiny but richly scented white flowers.	X
Paeonia lutea ludlowii TREE PAEONY	150×120 cm (5×4 ft)	Apr/May	Golden-yellow single flowers and decorative finely-cut leaves.	X
Philadelphus 'Belle Etoile' MOCK ORANGE	150×150 cm (5×5 ft)	June/July	An outstanding form with arching sprays of single white flowers.	F
Phlomis fruticosa JERUSALEM SAGE	100×120 cm (3×4 ft)	June/July	Grey-green woolly foliage makes a perfect foil for sulphur-yellow flower spikes.	X
Pieris forrestii FOREST FLAME	200×150 cm (6×5 ft)	Apr/May	Main attraction is the scarlet, poinsettia-like young growths. 'Wakehurst Form' has the most brilliant colouring.	X
Santolina chamaecyparissus 'Nana' COTTON LAVENDER	30×30 cm (1×1 ft)	Foliage	Finely cut silver foliage makes this an ideal subject for the edge of the border.	LW
Senecio laxifolius	50×100 cm (1½×3 ft)	Foliage	Useful grey-leaved shrubs that provide contrast in the border.	X
Syringa 'Katherine Havemeyer' LILAC	200×150 cm (6×5 ft)	May	One of the best double lilacs with large pyramidal flower trusses of deep purple. Very fragrant.	F

7·The Vegetable and Fruit Garden

Home-grown vegetables are not only tastier but infinitely fresher than the shop-bought kinds. Nothing can compare with a dish of peas or runner beans fresh from the garden or cabbages 'with the squeak still in 'em', as an old country gardener of my acquaintance used to describe them. However, it would scarcely be true to pretend that a vegetable garden can be made and looked after without a fair amount of work being involved, both in its initial preparation and subsequent maintenance.

Just the same, many gardeners, and especially those with families, may consider the effort involved a worthwhile one and there are ways of cutting down on unnecessary work. The most important rule is not to grow more crops or a greater variety than you can reasonably look after and maintain in a healthy, weed- and pest-free condition. Crop cultivation often entails more trouble than the initial preparation of the site.

The globe artichoke rates a place in any garden for the sheer beauty of its handsome grey-green coarsely toothed leaves, which are widely used for flower arranging. The plants reach a height of up to 1.5 m (5 ft), with a spread of equal dimensions. The large flower heads, like those of a king-sized thistle, are gathered while still at the bud stage. Cooked and served with melted butter, they make a dish fit for a king. Plants can be grown on for several years. After that they tend to deteriorate, but replace-

The rewards of a well-stocked kitchen garden. Careful planning and planting cut down on the work of cultivation.

ments are easily made simply by detaching any rooted side shoots from the parent plant.

It is possible to grow some vegetables without a garden, by using pots and other containers. The introduction of growing bags, filled with a suitable compost, has made the cultivation of tomatoes a virtually trouble-free operation. Even without a greenhouse or cold frame, tomatoes can be raised against a south- or west-facing wall. The bush and dwarf varieties need no support and are a boon to the busy gardener.

With the tomato varieties that need tying, the work can be simplified by using rings or plant ties that are slipped on to or twisted round the main stem and supporting cane.

The vegetable plot

When it comes to the more conventional ways of growing vegetables, there are various ways of saving labour, but real success in the kitchen garden cannot be achieved without work. Nevertheless, by sowing thinly in the first place, you can cut down the subsequent singling of vegetable plants to one operation rather than several. Tiny seeds, such as those of onion, can be mixed with sand or sown from a seed-sowing gadget so that they do not fall too thickly. Pelleted seeds of a number of vegetables, such as leeks, onions and lettuces, are also available.

The work entailed in successional sowing to provide a continuity of crops can be minimized by growing varieties that do not run to seed easily. With cabbages, a succession can be obtained easily by cross-cutting the stems after the heads have been harvested. The stumps will sprout again to provide a further supply of 'greens' after four to five weeks.

However hard-pressed for time you are, almost everyone can find the time for a few salad crops together with a row of runner beans and a few outdoor tomato plants.

For those who would like to be more ambitious and grow a representative selection of vegetables, the list that follows includes those that need the least attention. There will, of course, be the usual jobs of sowing, weeding and feeding and watering during dry spells.

Easy-to-grow vegetables
Artichokes, Jerusalem
These are extremely easy to grow, requiring no cultivation apart from periodic weeding. They make an effective summer screen with their tall, sunflower-like growths. They are particularly useful for camouflaging the compost heap or other similar unsightly garden objects. Artichoke tubers have a distinctive flavour and can provide an occasional alternative to potatoes. The tubers are planted in February, about 15 cm (6 in) apart, and are dug up as required from November to February.

Beans
Beans are one of the most valuable vegetable crops, and need very little attention after the initial preparation of the ground and can actually enrich the soil. Nitrogen-fixing bacteria in small nodules on their roots take in nitrogen gas from the air and convert it into valuable plant food; this is then made available to successive crops if the stem, leaves and roots of the beans are dug into the soil.

Preparation of the ground should be as thorough as possible; plenty of compost or well-rotted manure should be dug in a few weeks before the seed is sown.

Broad beans
The seed of broad beans can be sown in November to produce early crops the following spring. Further sowings should be made in February and March to provide continuity of supplies. The large seeds should be sown 25 cm (9 in) apart in two staggered rows, in shallow drills 6.5 cm (2½ in) deep and 15 cm (6 in) wide. 'Aquadulce' is one of the best for late autumn sowing. 'Masterpiece Green Longpod' is a green-seeded variety for sowing in February and March.

In exposed gardens where wind is likely to damage taller varieties, 'The Sutton' would be the best choice. This heavy-cropping dwarf broad bean grows only 30 cm (1 ft) tall and seed can be sown in succession from February to July.

French beans
Dwarf French beans are easy to grow and the busy gardener may prefer them to the runner beans. They will need no staking or pinching out and will produce heavy crops of tender beans over a long period. They also retain their flavour and texture better than 'runners' in the deep freeze. 'The Prince' and 'Masterpiece' are two good varieties. Seed can be sown from mid-April to mid-July, 5 cm (2 in) deep in double rows. The plants should be thinned to 20–30 cm (8–12 in) apart. Picking the beans while they are young and tender will help extend the cropping period.

Runner beans
Runner beans are one of the most popular and worthwhile of all vegetable crops. The easiest way of supporting the plants is to train them up 2.5 m (8 ft) bamboo canes; the canes are arranged wigwam fashion in groups of four, tying each group securely at the top. The wigwams should be in rows and about 45–60 cm (1–1½ ft) apart. Allow five or six plants per person. To obtain really heavy crops, deep digging and liberal manuring will be necessary, but runners will still produce adequate crops without this VIP treatment. The seed is sown outdoors in mid-May or in April; to ensure earlier cropping, cloches can be used to warm up the soil before sowing and left on until the seedlings are off to a good start. The seed should be sown 5 cm (2 in) deep, two seeds at the base of each cane. As the seedlings develop remove the weaker of the two.

Good varieties include 'Enorma', a really spectacular runner with pods up to 50 cm (20 in) long; 'Prizewinner', an exceptionally heavy cropper; and 'Streamline', an old favourite

The Kitchen Garden

● Slow-growing box hedge divides pleasure garden from kitchen garden. This type of hedge is particularly valuable since it does not block out the light or take up valuable space, and requires only occasional clipping.

● Crossing paved paths are simple to maintain and provide easy access to all plots, this is especially important when harvesting crops during wet or wintry weather.

● The garden is divided into five main plots. One main plot is used for long-term vegetables, e.g. globe artichokes, and those that do not need yearly rotation, e.g. onions and marrows. One plot is used solely for fruit, and the remaining three are ideal for simple crop rotation which is essential to prevent a build-up of soil-borne diseases.

● Fruit cage protects soft fruits from marauding birds.

● The tripod or wigwam system for growing runner beans is wind resistant and less likely to be blown down in bad weather. It also makes the best use of the limited space.

● Dwarf varieties of vegetables do not need any elaborate staking and they also take up less space than standard varieties.

● Potatoes grown under black polythene do not need earthing up. This method also suppresses weeds and conserves moisture.

● The choice of crops grown are those that can be used over a long period of time, for example, perpetual spinach, Brussels sprouts, purple sprouting broccoli, salad bowl lettuce, etc.

● Espalier, cordon or fan-trained fruit trees produce good crops but unlike standard forms do not take up valuable space or block out the light.

● Garden shed provides convenient storage for tools.

● Compost is easily accessible but unobtrusive. The addition of some form of lid will also keep out the rain.

Key:
1. Garden shed
2. Compost heap
3. Globe artichokes
4. Marrows and courgettes
5. Radish
6. Onions and shallots
7. Salad Bowl lettuce (cut-and-come again)
8. Fruit trees
9. Brussels sprouts
10. Curly kale
11. Purple sprouting broccoli
12. Cabbage
13. Cabbage lettuce 'Webb's Wonderful' (long-standing)
14. *Buxus* 'Suffruticosa' (Dwarf Box)
15. Perpetual spinach (Spinach Beet)
16. Beetroot
17. Carrot
18. Potatoes under black polythene
19. Runner beans
20. Dwarf French beans
21. Dwarf broad beans
22. Fruit cage protecting soft fruits.

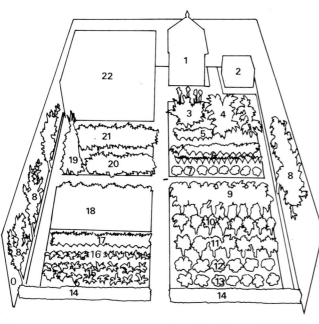

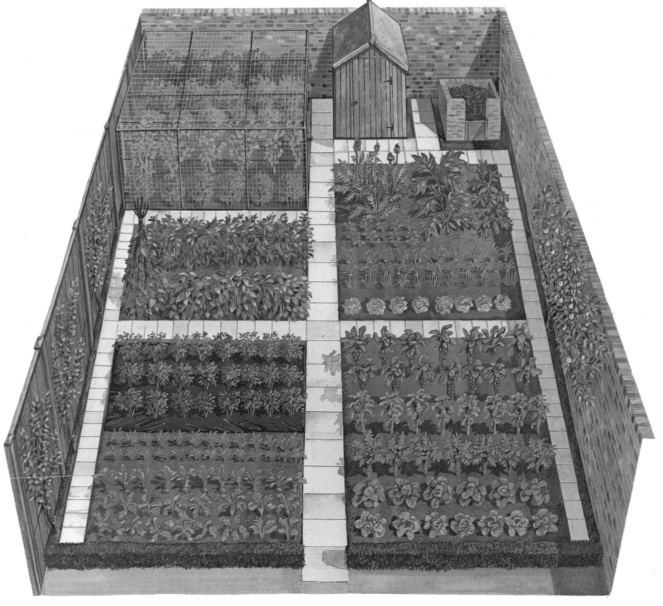

that is still widely grown. Most varieties of runner bean can also be grown successfully without staking, if the growing shoots are pinched out when they reach about 45 cm (1½ ft) tall. As well as saving a great deal of labour, this will also result in earlier crops, although the total yield will be less than from plants grown by more orthodox methods. 'Kelvedon Marvel' responds well to this treatment.

Beetroot

Choose the globe varieties, as these will grow well in any soil, as long as it does not dry out in summer. Pull the roots as needed, when they are young and succulent.

Sow the seed 5 cm (2 in) apart and 2.5 cm (1 in) deep in rows 30 cm (1 ft) apart from late April to mid-July, thinning the seedlings to 10–15 cm (4–6 in) apart. Any roots still in the ground in late autumn can be lifted and stored in boxes of sand, peat or sifted soil through the winter months, provided they are protected from frost. 'Detroit', specially bred for summer sowing and quick maturing, is one of the best varieties.

Broccoli, Sprouting

This is a trouble-free crop that will provide you with regular supplies of 'greens' over a long period. Seed is sown outdoors in May, about 13 mm (½ in) deep. The seedlings are planted out in June or July, 45 cm (1½ ft) apart in rows 60 cm (2 ft) apart.

Calabrese, which produces its large green heads, or 'spears', in August and September, is one of the best of the brassica crops for freezing. The delicious spears retain their flavour to a greater extent than most other green vegetables at sub-zero temperatures. 'Autumn Spear' is one of the best varieties.

Cabbage

Much time and trouble can be saved by sowing cabbage seed where the plants are to stand, thinning the seedlings to 15 cm (6 in) apart when the first pair of true leaves develops, and later using alternate plants as 'greens' when they start to jostle their neighbours. For this purpose a quick-maturing cabbage, such as 'Golden Acre' is most suitable. Grown in this way, a spring sowing will produce cabbages ready for cutting in late summer or early autumn.

Seed should be sown 15 mm (½ in) deep in rich fertile soil. Before the seed is sown, plenty of well-rotted manure or compost should be dug into the soil, and acid soils should have a dressing of lime (enough to whiten the surface) forked into the top spit. Where organic fertilizers are not available, the ground should be dressed with a general fertilizer, such as Growmore, at the rate of 60g/m² (2oz/sq yd) a week before the seed is sown. If cabbage root fly is a problem, an application of calomel dust or bromophos in the seed drills and around the seedlings when they are thinned will guard against attacks.

If you want to grow cabbage in a more orthodox way, the choice of varieties is wide. However, two sowings should produce a succession sufficient to supply the requirements of a family of four. The seedlings should be transplanted when they have four true leaves to stand 30–40 cm (12–15 in) apart each way. In spring, sow popular kinds such as 'Christmas Drumhead' or 'Winnigstadt' to mature in autumn and winter. Autumn sowings of 'Wheeler's Imperial' or 'Harbinger' will provide supplies of 'greens' in spring.

Buying cabbage plants ready to be planted out will save time and labour, but there is the added risk of importing club root disease.

Lettuce

Good crisp, succulent lettuce that will stand well without running to seed must be watered regularly during dry periods. By careful planning and the use of cloches and cold frames, it is possible to have home-grown lettuce practically the whole year round. Busy gardeners, however, will doubtless prefer to save labour by growing only two or three varieties that will provide them with fresh lettuce during summer and autumn. Among such varieties, 'Tom Thumb' and 'Little Gem', both old favourites, rank very highly. The former is a dwarf cabbage lettuce with a tight solid head. It matures exceptionally fast. Little Gem is also compact, and is intermediate between a cabbage and cos type.

Of the newer introductions, I particularly like 'Sigmadeep', a dark green butterhead lettuce, of upright growth, with few outside leaves and a crisp tender heart. A bonus for those with small gardens is the fact that its narrow shape allows the plants to be spaced more closely than other kinds of butterhead lettuce.

The crisp-hearted kinds of lettuce which are particularly resistant to bolting (running to seed prematurely) are good for middle and late summer, particularly in dry conditions. 'Windermere' and 'Webb's Wonderful' are both slow to run to seed, even in times of drought, provided they are kept watered.

'Salad Bowl', popular on the Continent, is a cut-and-come-again variety with little or no waste, and a boon to busy gardeners. It is a nonhearting variety that produces abundant supplies of curled leaves over a long period. Ideally these should be picked while still young and tender.

Lettuce seed should be sown thinly in drills 15 mm (½ in) deep and 30 cm (1 ft) apart. As soon as two true leaves appear, thin to a distance of 15–30 cm (6–12 in) apart, depending on the size of the variety.

Marrows

Choosing a bush variety of marrow will save not only space but also the work of pinching out runners and side shoots. Plants are easily raised from seed, sown in groups of two or three where they are to remain. Each group should be 60 cm (2 ft) apart, and the seedlings thinned to a single plant at each position as soon as they have their first pair of true leaves. Marrows need rich soil and plenty of water. They should be harvested young, when they have a much finer flavour. Such treatment also results in longer and more prolific cropping.

Two varieties well worth growing are 'Green Bush Improved' and 'White Bush'. Both are good croppers, producing marrows of moderate size and excellent flavour.

For courgettes, sow the varieties 'Green Bush', 'Zucchini', or 'Golden Zucchini', all of which produce mini-marrows in abundance. Courgettes should be picked when they are only 10–15 cm (4–6 in) long.

Onions

The easiest way of growing onions is from 'sets'. These are small bulblets,

Globe artichokes: an easily grown luxury.

grown especially for planting out. The sets are planted just below the surface with only the tips of the bulblets showing, 10–15 cm (4–6 in) apart in rows 30 cm (1 ft) apart, during February or March. If any sets work loose (or are pulled out by birds) simply press them back into the soil.

Equally easy to cultivate are shallots. These should be planted during January or February in a similar manner to onion sets. Instead of producing a single bulb, like the latter, they divide to make a cluster of bulbs. The flavour of shallots is milder than that of onions and the smaller bulbs are useful for pickling.

The crops can be harvested in August, when the leaves die off. Onions and shallots should be stored in dry airy conditions. Properly looked after, they will keep until the following year's crops are ready.

Peas

Peas gathered fresh from the garden and cooked with a sprig of mint and a pinch of sugar have an exquisite flavour that shop-bought varieties cannot rival. Most varieties of peas also freeze well, retaining much of their original flavour and texture. As with beans, the remains of the plants after harvesting will enrich the soil if they are dug into it (see page 68).

The main labour involved in growing them is the provision of some kind of support. Twiggy pea sticks or plastic or wire netting are two of the supports usually adopted. The latter is easier to set up and take down, and can be used again year after year. However, even this work can be saved if dwarf varieties are chosen, since these can be grown without support, although they will crop better if provided with pea sticks.

Peas like rich soil conditions, so the site should be prepared by digging in plenty of well-rotted manure or garden compost during the autumn or winter before sowing. They will also benefit from a dressing of lime, at a rate determined by the result of a soil test (see page 11). The lime must be applied a month before manuring.

Sow the seed in flat drills about 15 cm (6 in) wide, at a depth of 5–8 cm (2–3 in), according to whether the soil is light or heavy. There should be about 8 seeds per 30 cm (1 ft) of drill. Rows should be anything from 60–120 cm (2–4 ft) apart, depending on variety; a good rule of thumb is to allow a space between rows equal to the ultimate height of the plants.

Early varieties, sown during March and April, will crop in about 12 weeks. Second earlies are ready for picking a week or so later, closely followed by the maincrop varieties.

Sowings of early varieties made right up until the beginning of June will produce successive crops until early autumn.

In the following list of recommended varieties, the earlies and second earlies need little or no support, while the maincrops must always have support. All can be deep frozen, but those marked (F) are particularly suitable for this purpose.
Earlies: 'Pioneer', 'Little Marvel' (F), 'Feltham First' and 'Kelvedon Wonder' (F). 'Meteor' is an extra-hardy variety that can be sown outdoors from November to January for early crops the following spring. These varieties grow about 45 cm (1½ ft) tall.
Second Earlies: 'Fek', 'Onward' (F). These grow to about 60 cm (2 ft) tall.
Maincrops: 'Lord Chancellor', 'Hurst Green Shaft' (F), 'Senator'. These grow to a height of about 90 cm (3 ft).

Potatoes

The average vegetable plot is not large enough to grow sufficient quantities of potatoes to last the whole year through. Most people, however, like to find room for a few rows of earlies. These will not need earthing up and will be ready for use when potatoes are at their most expensive in the shops.

Early potatoes can be planted towards the end of March, but not during periods of heavy frost or when the soil is waterlogged. The tubers should go in 38 cm (15 in) apart and 10–15 cm (4–6 in) deep, and the rows need be only 60 cm (2 ft) apart. 'Arran Pilot' is a good early variety but conditions vary and you should consult a local supplier.

If you decide to grow maincrop potatoes, you could save yourself a lot of work by growing them under sheets of black polythene. The tubers are planted in the usual way, but as soon as the shoots appear, sheets of black polythene are stretched over the bed with cross-shaped slits cut in them for the plants to grow through. The sheets should be anchored at the edges under a layer of soil. Grown in this way, potatoes will need no earthing up or weeding, and as an extra bonus, the polythene will help keep the soil moist in dry weather. Maincrop varieties: 'Majestic', 'King Edward', 'Golden Wonder'.

Radish

Everyone can find space for a few sowings of this useful salad crop. Early sowings given the protection of a cold frame or cloches in February will mature in four or five weeks. These can be followed by outdoor sowings in March and April. In July you can sow winter radish, with roots the size of a golf ball; these are excellent for slicing as an ingredient of winter salads.

Sow the seed 15 mm (½ in) deep in drills 23 cm (9 in) apart for winter radish, and 15 cm (6 in) apart for other varieties. Thin winter radishes to 15 cm (6 in) apart, and other sorts to 5 cm (2 in) apart as soon as they are large enough to handle.

For outdoor sowing, 'French Breakfast', 'Scarlet Globe' and 'Red Prince' are suitable. Two good varieties of winter radish are 'Black Spanish Round' and 'China Rose'.

Turnip

This is a useful crop to sow in June and July for winter use, preferably on a site where early peas or spring cabbage have been growing. Before

sowing, give a light dressing (about 60 g per sq m/2 oz per sq yd) of a general fertilizer to supplement the residue of plant foods left by the previous crop. The seed is sown in drills 15 mm (½ in) deep and 30 cm (1 ft) apart, and the seedlings are thinned to 10–15 cm (4–6 in) when large enough to handle. Good varieties are 'Golden Ball' and 'Snowball'.

Growing and Pruning Fruit

The rewards of cultivating a fruit garden are well worth the modest effort involved. The main operations consist of pruning, spraying and feeding.

Pruning, of both soft and tree fruits, is a relatively simple job, once the basic rules have been mastered, and becomes progressively less time-consuming as the trees come to maturity.

Spraying techniques have been greatly simplified, with the numerous multi-purpose sprays now available cutting down on the work involved. If you buy only healthy, disease-free plants and look after them well, with luck you should not need to spend much time on spraying (see pages 75–77).

Enriching the soil well with garden compost, manure or other sources of humus at planting time will cut down on the need for feeding later. Mulching with humus-rich materials, plus annual applications of fertilizer, will take care of subsequent feeding.

To cut down on labour further, soft fruits should be grown in a cage. This is the easiest and most effective way of protecting crops from birds.

If you haven't enough space for a proper fruit plot, you could grow some fruit trees in the ornamental garden. An apple or pear tree in blossom is just as beautiful as the flowering crabapples, Japanese cherries and other trees chosen solely for their appearance.

Fruit Trees

With the older kinds of fruit tree, pruning could be a long and arduous job, necessitating the use of ladders, long-handled pruners and so on. The average present-day garden is not large enough to accommodate this type of tree, so that nowadays most

gardeners grow varieties that are grafted on to special dwarfing rootstocks.

This makes pruning simpler and an added advantage with this type of tree is that it fruits much sooner. Growing apples and pears in espalier and cordon form has already been mentioned under Hedging (page 41), but there are other types of dwarf tree that can be just as useful in the small garden.

The most prolific cropper and the easiest to manage of these is the bush form. Apples and pears in this form should be planted 3–4.5 m (10–15 ft) apart, in rows 2.5–3 m (8–10 ft) apart. Plums and cherries will need rather more space than this.

Pyramid trees, which are only slightly less labour-saving than the bush type, consist of a central main stem with progressively shortened side branches that give the tree its tapering pyramidal shape. These would be a good choice where a number of different varieties are to be grown. They can be planted as little as 1–1.2 m (3½–4 ft) apart, in rows 2.5–3 m (8–10 ft) apart. Pruning to maintain the shape is not quite such a simple operation as it is with bush trees, because the side branches must be shortened annually to maintain the tapering outline. Apart from certain varieties of plums and greengages, this form is suited mainly to apples and pears, which, as mentioned above, can also be obtained in cordon form (the most space-saving type of all).

All the types of tree mentioned are obtainable in bush form, as are cherries. Generally speaking, however, sweet cherries are not worth the labour involved, owing to the difficulty in protecting the fruit from birds. Morello cherry trees in fan-trained form are a better proposition. They crop well against a north wall and the fruit can be easily netted. Maintaining the fan structure, however, calls for a fair amount of pruning.

Where fruit is concerned, the choice of suitable varieties is of great importance. Most apples and pears need another variety to fertilize them properly, although some of the so-called 'self-fertile' ones will produce quite good crops on their own. To overcome the difficulties of cross-fertilization in a very small garden, a 'family tree' can be grown. On such trees, several different varieties are grafted on to a single rootstock.

The drawback with these trees, however, lies in the difficulty in pruning. The different varieties will need varying treatments if the balance of the tree is to be maintained, and if a takeover by the most vigor-ous variety is to be avoided.

When fruit trees are first planted, the only pruning needed is the cutting out of any obviously dead wood and stems that are crossing or growing into the centre. After that, until growth starts to slow down as the trees reach maturity, annual pruning will consist, in general, of shortening main shoots by one third and cutting back laterals (side shoots) to two or three buds to encourage the development of fruiting spurs.

Plums and cherries are pruned in late summer, as soon as the fruit has been gathered. Winter pruning of plums is not advisable, owing to their

This fan-trained apple tree is easy to prune and produces a good early crop.

susceptibility to silver leaf disease.

Soft fruits

All the various pruning procedures for soft fruits are easy to carry out and none of them involves much time or labour.

Blackcurrants bear all their fruit on stems which were formed during the previous year. Because of this, they should be pruned immediately after the fruit has been gathered or during the following autumn and winter. Old growths should either be cut out altogether or shortened by one third, depending on the number of new young replacement shoots available.

In contrast to blackcurrants, red and white currants bear their fruit on short 'fruiting spurs' which develop on the older wood as well as

Red currants should be spur-pruned annually, so that the spurs (side-shoots) will produce plenty of fruit.

on the new, young wood. Pruning, therefore, consists of cutting back all side shoots each winter to within 2.5 cm (1 in) of the main stems. This will encourage the formation of fruiting spurs. The main branches can be allowed to grow until the desired height is reached – usually about 1.2–1.5 m (4–5 ft).

Both red and white currants can also be grown as cordons. To prune cordon red and white currants, shorten the laterals (the side shoots that grow out at an angle from the main shoots, or 'leaders') to five or six leaves from the base during summer. In late autumn of the same year, prune these back further to two

or three buds from the base. Leave the leaders unpruned until they have reached the top wire.

Gooseberries are also easy to prune. The method is similar to that for bush apples, and entails the removal of old and dead growths and pruning to keep the centre of the bush open; this will admit light and air and allow you to pick the fruit without being pricked by the sharp thorns. Gooseberries can also be grown as cordons; prune these by shortening all the laterals to three buds from the base and cutting back the leaders when they have reached the desired height.

With both bush and cordon forms, prune your gooseberries in early winter, unless birds are a problem, when you should wait until the buds break.

Raspberries, loganberries and blackberries fruit on canes of the previous year's growth. Once they have fruited, the current season's canes die off and these should be cut out as soon as possible. The best of the new young canes – about six to each plant – can then be tied in as replacements and the rest pruned out.

Blackberries and loganberries will need tying in to wires, strained horizontally to stout posts at 60 cm (2 ft) intervals. The busy gardener may prefer to concentrate on raspberries. By stretching the horizontal wires in pairs, about 5 cm (2 in) apart, tying can be avoided since the raspberry canes can be trained through the two wires without any other support.

Although it does not strictly fall under the heading of pruning, the removal of runners from strawberries is an operation which it seems appropriate to deal with here. A runner is an aerial stem that roots at its tip when it touches moist soil, and forms a new plant. Strawberries produce masses of runners each summer, when the crop will be covered by netting to prevent birds taking the ripening fruit. Although it may be a little tedious lifting off and replacing the netting, you should remove any runners as soon as they appear (because they use food that would otherwise go towards swelling the fruit) – unless of course you want to increase your stock. Take care to propagate only from strong healthy plants.

8 · Pests and Diseases

A great deal of wasted effort can be avoided if you take the correct preventative measures against plant pests and diseases. If such problems are tackled when they are first noticed, it will save the extra time and trouble involved in getting rid of them once they have become firmly established. Prevention is always better than cure.

It is often possible to avoid the time, trouble, expense and hazards of using pesticides by following these common-sense rules. Firstly, you should ensure that you give your plants the best conditions so that they grow strong and healthy and thus have more chance of resisting attacks by pests and diseases.

Secondly, you should choose disease-resistant plants whenever possible – for example, there are tomato varieties that are resistant to cladosporium disease, and wilt-resistant asters – although this applies to relatively few plants only.

Thirdly, if you buy in any plants from nurseries or garden centres, make sure that they are guaranteed free from pests or diseases. It is pointless taking precautions if you then introduce trouble from outside.

Finally, it is essential to practise good garden hygiene. Prunings, for example, should always be burnt. Never leave them lying about under trees and bushes and do not put them on the compost heap. Diseased material is a common cause of infection in the garden.

Any garden rubbish, in fact, that is

A mechanized leaf-sweeper cuts down on the work of tidying up in autumn.

not suitable for composting should be burned as soon as possible. Burning kills disease spores and the resulting ash is a valuable source of potash for your plants.

The bottoms of hedges should be cleared out regularly and dead leaves swept up and composted as soon as possible after they have fallen. These are both common sources of plant and pest infestation. Patches of long grass and weeds, too, provide ideal breeding places for slugs and snails.

In recent years there has been a strong reaction against the use of many pesticides on environmental grounds, and it is very important to avoid the indiscriminate use of these chemical poisons and to confine their use as far as possible to those that break down after use to harmless substances and which do not harm wildlife.

Great care should be taken when any garden chemicals are used. The makers' instructions should be strictly adhered to and careful heed paid to their warnings. Above all, keep them out of the reach of children in a locked cupboard and in their original containers – not in soft drinks bottles.

The safest pesticides are manufactured from natural ingredients. They are pyrethrum, obtained from the pyrethrum plant, derris (or rotenone), extracted from the roots of a tropical plant, and quassia, obtained from the wood of a South American tree. Quassia was formerly supplied in the form of chips for soaking in water to produce a liquid insecticide. Nowadays, it is obtainable in liquid form for making up into a spray. Pyrethrum is obtainable as a spray concentrate, while derris can be bought either as a dust in handy 'puffer packs' or as a spray concentrate. A mixture of pyrethrum and derris is also available, which is more effective at destroying pests than either pesticide alone.

Between them, these organic materials will control a large number of garden pests, including aphids (greenfly and blackfly), caterpillars, thrips, flea beetles and the grubs of the raspberry beetle. A small hand sprayer will be adequate for applying them in the average garden. They can be safely used on any garden or greenhouse plant and leave no long-lasting toxic residues to harm wild-life, pets or humans.

However, it is important to remember that derris will kill fish, so on no account spray anywhere near a pond or stream. You should avoid killing bees and other beneficial insects when using derris or pyrethrum by spraying after sunset when these creatures are no longer on the wing.

Another natural way of coping with pests, in which a good deal of interest has been shown in recent years, is by growing special plants in association with vegetable crops to repel the particular pests to which they are susceptible. The best-known example of this is the planting of French or African marigolds in the greenhouse to prevent infestations of whitefly, one of the most trouble-some greenhouse pests. I must admit that I have always been a trifle sceptical of such remedies, but I have given this method a trial for the past two seasons and, whatever the reason, there has been no sign of whitefly, whereas in previous years, my tomatoes and cucumbers have been plagued by these pests, which were impossible to control without constant recourse to chemical sprays.

Other similar plant associations include the growing of summer savory with broad beans to discourage the attacks of blackfly, to which they are usually so prone; chervil with radish as a protection against borers and

Spray only when necessary and always obey the manufacturer's instructions.

weevils; and sage or thyme with carrots and cabbage. Both the cabbage moth and the cabbage white butterfly are also repelled.

For further details on safe methods of pest control, many of which are in the long run labour (and money) saving, consult one of the many excellent books on organic gardening, and write to the Henry Doubleday Research Association, Convent Lane, Bocking, Braintree, Essex.

If you have a serious attack of a pest, and the safer alternatives given above are not working, then as a last resort you could consider using one of the less harmful modern pesticides. Systemic insecticides and fungicides penetrate into the sap of plants and remain active for a week or more. They are extremely effective against sap-sucking insects, such as aphids (greenfly and blackfly), thrips and leafhoppers.

Systemic fertilizers can be mixed with foliar feeds to combine two spraying operations in one. Application is best made by some form of pressure spray but for the very small garden, a syringe with a fine nozzle should be adequate.

Benlate is a systemic fungicide that controls many disease conditions, including grey mould, tomato leaf mould and powdery mildew, as well as black spot on roses.

For potato and other blight diseases, the chemical Dithane 945, for many years used in agriculture, is very effective. It also controls other diseases such as rust, leaf spot, downy mildew, apple scab and peach leaf curl. However, potato blight should be easily controlled by spraying with Bordeaux mixture, a safer alternative to Dithane 945. Safer still, grow a blight-resistant variety such as 'Majestic' or 'Pentland Crown'.

Particular care is needed when treating crops in the greenhouse, and an insecticide based on the chemical resmethrin can be safely used against green and whitefly. In fact the manufacturers claim that crops can be gathered and eaten on the same day they are sprayed.

Top right: Aphids can be controlled by spraying with pyrethrum or a systemic insecticide. Bottom right: Grow summer savory as a companion plant with broad beans to discourage blackfly.

9·Gardening for the Disabled

In recent years, a great deal has been done to help the disabled, elderly and infirm to participate more fully in the pleasures of gardening. A number of manufacturers produce specialized tools and appliances for the disabled and there are a number of demonstration gardens throughout the British Isles, including those of the Disabled Living Foundation in Battersea Park and Syon Park, as well as the Royal Horticultural Society's special garden for the disabled at Wisley.

Disabilities range from the backaches and stresses of the elderly to the almost total immobility of those crippled by illness or accident. For those in the first category, only slight adaptations may be needed, including the choice of more suitable tools and the use of proprietary kneeling devices which will minimize stooping and bending as well as doubling as useful garden stools when they are reversed.

The more seriously disabled or infirm will usually need a specially planned and designed garden in order to be able to pursue their hobby in relative comfort. Many disabled people possess tremendous determination and, as a result, devise ingenious methods enabling them to take full advantage of any such aids available to make gardening easier.

Planning for the Disabled

The design of a garden for disabled persons will depend, to a large extent, on whether they are able to walk or are confined to wheelchairs.

For the elderly the infirm who are still able to walk, the provision of handrails and non-slip paths is of the utmost importance. Also, wherever possible, steps should be replaced by gently sloping ramps.

Handrails, which should be provided alongside the main paths, can be constructed of wood, steel or plastic tubing. For safety's sake, extra care should be taken in their installation. Only if they are really safe and firm can they be used with complete confidence. A rickety support is exceedingly dangerous and, for the old and frail, can be worse than no support at all.

Paths should be surfaced with asphalt or non-slip paving stones. This is of the utmost importance where the garden is designed for the walking disabled, since it is essential to provide a safe surface not only for those who have to use walking frames or similar aids, but also for those with lesser disabilities that make walking difficult.

Paving stones are obtainable in a wide range of sizes, shapes and colours and most of them have non-slip surfaces. To prevent any subsequent movement, the slabs should be laid in cement and be properly levelled, with great care taken to avoid even the slightest irregularities. (See pages 21-24.)

Paths should be at least 1 m (3 ft) wide, to allow for the passage of wheelchairs or to permit a disabled person and his helper to walk two abreast. For wheelchairs, it will be necessary to provide turning spaces at strategic intervals and these should not be less than 1.2–1.5 m (4–5 ft) in width.

In addition to paths running through the garden, supplementary paths running through beds and borders will be particularly useful, for these will allow easy access to all cultivated areas for any necessary maintenance work. For those confined to wheelchairs and for the elderly and infirm who are unable to bend or stoop, raised beds are the best answer.

Planting

The larger beds, especially those at ground level, are best planted with easy-to-maintain shrubs, with an under-planting of ground cover, as described in previous sections of the book (see pages 31–35 and 64–65). If regular mulching is also carried out, beds of this kind will require only a minimum of attention apart from an occasional pruning of the shrubs. Between them, the ground cover plants and the mulches will smother the majority of annual and perennial weeds.

Raised beds for the disabled gardener can be constructed from a variety of materials – brick, walling stone, natural stone or peat. Peat is particularly suitable where the gardener wishes to grow lime-hating subjects such as rhododendrons, azaleas, camellias and heathers on a site with predominantly alkaline soil, since the beds can be filled with peat, which is non-alkaline.

Another point in favour of peat blocks is the fact that they are so light to handle. They will need a thorough soaking before use, after which they can be bonded like bricks until the required height of wall is reached. This can vary according to the needs of the person concerned, but approximately 1 m (3 ft) should be optimum, both for those who can walk and for those in wheelchairs.

Raised beds can be laid out to form attractive designs, suitable for large or small areas, as the illustration showing the Royal Horticultural Society's Garden for the Disabled at Wisley, shows so well. Such beds can have as many and varied uses as those in the more conventional kind of garden, and can be adapted to suit individual needs.

The 'Gardens for the Disabled' Trust of Headcorn Manor, Headcorn, Kent, TN27 9NP offer their own specially designed aids to easier gardening. They are constructed of fibreglass, which makes them light and easy to handle. They include a system of raised bed units which are obtainable in sizes ranging from 1.2×1.6 m (4×5½ ft) up to 1.2×5 m (4×17 ft). These are designed to be comfortable to work at from either a wheelchair or garden stool. The soil depth varies from 10 cm (4 in) at the edges to 45 cm (18 in) or more at the centre.

Also obtainable are smaller circular plant containers of similar height with a circular top 60 cm (2 ft) in diameter. These can either be planted up or used as containers for pot plants.

Tools for Disabled Gardeners

Many of the conventional garden tools can be comfortably used by the disabled, but there are others designed specially with their needs in mind. These include a weeder that looks like a walking stick, with a spear-shaped end and a lever action which enables the end to grip the weed prior to pulling it out. This is a useful tool for the removal of deep-rooted weeds such as docks and dandelions. Shallow-rooted annual weeds can be removed with a long-handled rake-like weeder, the blades of which drag the weeds out of the soil. The latter tool also comes with a short handle for use at closer quarters on raised beds.

Cut-and-hold flower gatherers, both long and short-handled, make the task of deadheading easy; there are also long-handled appliances for picking up piles of weeds and other garden rubbish without needing to bend down at all.

Above: Raised beds make work easier for the disabled. Below: Design for the disabled at the RHS Gardens, Wisley.

Other useful tools include trowel, fork and planter sets with special 'trigger' grips that enable those with stiff or disabled wrists or hands to grasp them firmly, and a spade and fork with spring-loaded shaft and blade that takes much of the effort out of digging – no bending or lifting of the spade is required.

Index

(Figures in italics refer to illustrations)

ACKNOWLEDGEMENTS
The publishers wish to thank the following organizations and individuals for their kind permission to reproduce the photographs in this book.

A–Z Botanical Collection Ltd. 24, 48, 49, 77 below right; Bernard Alfieri 25, 75, 79, below; Ardea (I.R. Beames) 30–31, (Sue Gooders) 62; Pat Brindley 1, 33, 45; Eric Crichton 32 below; Valerie Finnis 20–21; Susan Griggs Agency Ltd. (Michael Boys) 2–3, 4–5; The Iris Hardwick Library 32 above; George Hyde 35, 40, 44, 47, 52, 53, 77 above right; Leslie Johns & Associates 50–51; Harry Smith Horticultural Photographic Collection Ltd. 10–11, 14, 38, 39, 42–43, 46, 55, 56, 58, 61, 63, 66–67, 71, 72, 74, 76, 79 above right; Suttons Seeds Ltd., Torquay 28–29; Pamla Toler 15; Michael Warren 36–37.